GANBARU

How All Japan Pro Wrestling Survived the Year 2000 Roster Split

Jonathan Foye

Copyright © 2022 Jonathan Foye

All rights reserved

No part of this book may be reproduced, or transmitted in any form or by any means, electronic, mechanical, photocopying, recording, or otherwise, without express written permission of the publisher.

Cover art by Mushkilah

For Sarah and James

FOREWORD

This is a book about *puroresu*, professional wrestling in Japanese, written by a non-Japanese. This is a book about the intriguing world of professional wrestling written by a scholar. This is a book about sport, entertainment, culture, and humanity.

Professional wrestling was one of the first forms of American popular culture introduced to Japan after World War ll. There was the war. There was Pearl Harbor in 1941. There were Hiroshima and Nagasaki in 1945. Then, professional wrestling came to Japan in September of 1951, six years after the war, or just three weeks after the San Francisco Peace Treaty to be exact.

Mid-West-based wrestler-promoter Bobby Bruns and his tour group of seven American professional wrestlers travelled to Japan and performed a series of tribute shows for the American troops and GHQ (General Headquarters). The show included Rikidōzan, a former sumo wrestling star, who made his debut as an American style professional wrestler after three short weeks of training under Bruns' guidance. The seed was planted for the birth of puroresu.

The beginning of television and the beginning of puroresu were synonymous in Japan. Television helped Rikidōzan become a household name, and Rikidōzan's wrestling helped televisions become a popular household item. The network stations have always carried wrestling programs, which means Japan's wrestling business has always had the financial backing of the networks' mega budgets for their events. Rikidōzan was a superhero of black and white television.

Fast-forward a decade or two, and the Japanese economy had blossomed. Television's picture was now full living colour. Giant Baba and Antonio Inoki, Rikidōzan's two best pupils, had become the two kings of the wrestling industry. Baba founded AJPW (All Japan Pro Wrestling) and Inoki launched NJPW (New Japan Pro Wrestling) respectively in 1972. Two kings who each had their own company. Nippon Television (NTV) carried AJPW, and TV Asahi carried NJPW, thus forming two major leagues of puroresu.

The author of this book, Jonathan Foye, started following professional wrestling, like many others, during the Attitude era. He watched WWE's Bret

Hart fight Steve Austin in 1996, in a technical match, and was hooked on the idea that wrestling could be presented as a sport. He has been obsessed with it since. He started reading wrestling magazines that covered Japan and following superstar Tajiri and other Japanese stars in WWE. Some of the Internet forums he frequented had matches he could download, including the famous Misawa/Kawada match. He was stunned by the crowd reactions, and the way that some sections of the match were incredibly different to WWE's presentation.

Jonathan studied Communications, majoring in Journalism at Western Sydney University. He did the honours program, which made him think academia could be his career pathway. He undertook his PhD in Communications from 2011 to 2016, focusing on the methodology of critical discourse analysis. He is a part-time lecturer/tutor at the University of New South Wales and also now edits Insights magazine for the Uniting Church in Australia.

He remembers reading about the AJPW/Pro Wrestling NOAH split back in 2000 in American wrestling publications and being fascinated by it but not entirely understanding the cause. He found the big split so interesting, because the way a company could hold itself together despite the loss of most of its roster clearly required some strategic methodology and mental capacity.

Again, this is a book about wrestling/puroresu. It is also a book about sport, entertainment, culture, and humanity. Foye's fine piece of work can be read like J.D. Salinger's, Charles Baudelaire's, or even William Shakespeare's works. Let's enjoy.

Fumi Saito

Wrestling journalist and historian, sociologist, and a friend.

ABOUT THE AUTHOR

Jonathan Foye is a journalist and academic. He is the current Editor of *Insights* Magazine for the Uniting Church in NSW and the ACT. He holds a PhD in Communications and tutors part time at the University of New South Wales. Jonathan enjoys running, watching pro wrestling, and playing videogames. He lives in the Blue Mountains with his wife, Sarah, their son, James, and their Labrador, Walter. *Ganbaru* is his first book.

INTRODUCTION

The Japanese word *Ganbaru* literally means 'stand firm' when translated into English. In its context, it is often used to encourage people to continue to power through difficult or challenging times.

The term could so often have been used in All Japan Pro Wrestling over the past twenty-plus years, but perhaps never more so than during the period immediately after the promotion's infamous split in the year 2000. That split marked an end of an era for a company that was on top of the wrestling industry a few years prior.

As Matt Alt writes in *Pure Invention*, Japan has long been ahead of the curve in anticipating pop culture trends. From Sony's Walkman to videogames to the sheer ubiquity of the Hello Kitty brand, it has long acted as a trendsetter for western nations to follow[1].

While Alt's work does not address professional wrestling explicitly, the thesis could just as easily apply to Japan's take on the sport. Since the 1950s, when Rikidōzan was the sport's biggest star, *pur-*

oresu has combined the tropes of American pro wrestling with Sumo culture and created a product that is both unique and trendsetting for other parts of the world.

During the 1990s, for example, All Japan Pro Wrestling was widely regarded as the best pro wrestling company in the world. Operating since 1972, the company was formed by pro wrestling legend Giant Baba. A favourite of the mid-1990s tape trading scene, All Japan brought the unique, hard-hitting King's Road style of pro wrestling to the masses, with crazy bumps and cleverly laid out matches. With the likes of Mitsuharu Misawa, Akira Taue, Kenta Kobashi, and Tokashi Kawada churning out five-star matches, and young stars like Jun Akiyama on the rise, 1990s All Japan was on a record-making streak, selling out big arenas.

The promotion enjoyed its reputation as *the* place for international wrestlers to work, thanks to a low-stress environment, generous pay offs, and plenty of time off between tours. Simply put, All Japan was on top of the wrestling world and seemed destined to remain there for years to come.

Only a few years later, the promotion was at death's door. Clashes between company president Mitsuharu Misawa and owner Motoko Baba revolved around the direction the company should take. In 2000, the vast majority of All Japan's roster left with Misawa to form a new promotion, Pro Wrestling NOAH, leaving behind only two members of the permanent roster.

What happened next is one of the greatest comebacks in the history of pro wrestling.

Ganbaru is the story of All Japan Pro Wrestling's rise, fall, and recovery. It focuses on the way that All Japan survived what looked like the end of the company, with help from a prodigal champion and an old rival.

It is a story with lessons for the corporate world on how to be resilient during testing times as well as how to manage a full-blown crisis. It is also an exploration of recent history of the sport, which reveals much about how Japan's pro wrestling industry came to take its current shape.

Filling a gap

This book aims to fill a gap. While there has certainly been much written on the subject of the 2000 split and the impact it had on All Japan, no book has yet been entirely devoted to the subject of the split itself. Instead, articles in wrestling magazines and websites, books devoted to other subjects (such as Chris Charlton's excellent *Eggshells*, which explores the history of wrestling at the Tokyo Dome), and translations of Japanese publications have told the story in a piecemeal way.

Ganbaru aims to clear up a few misconceptions that have circulated in the years following the split. Fumi Saito is a veteran Japanese journalist, who has written about wrestling for decades. In an interview conducted for this book, Saito said the events surrounding the All Japan split have been subject to, 'lots of hearsay'. As someone who was entrenched in the Japanese wrestling industry, Saito is uniquely placed to dispel such misunderstandings, and *Ganbaru* draws on his memories, alongside others who were close to the events described.

The story surrounding the All Japan split is a fascinating one with many different layers. This story can be read through multiple lenses; as a tale of how grief and family resentments managed to nearly bring down a wrestling dynasty; as a lesson in crisis management for companies to consider; or simply as a series of connected events that explain for wrestling fans why the current landscape is the way it is.

That said, *Ganbaru* does not purport or aim to be an exhaustive history of the split, or the 'last word' on the events it explores. Instead, through a combination of research and original interviews, the book aims to add to what is already widely known about the events.

While *Ganbaru* largely focuses on All Japan and the impact the split had on that promotion, it does not seek to 'take sides' in its examination of the dispute between Motoko Baba and Mitsaharu Misawa. Rather, it explores the events of 2000 with an eye to the dynamics at play.

This includes looking at the central figures at the heart of the controversy as complex human beings dealing with grief over Giant Baba's death and the divide between Motoko Baba's desire to conserve the company he created and Misawa's intent to modernise its wrestling product.

Ganbaru was written for three broad audiences.

The first of these are fans of Japanese pro wrestling who are already well aware of the events surrounding the split and who want to learn more about how it happened, or where common misconceptions occur. These engaged readers will take away new information and anecdotes.

The second group are readers who are interested in pro wrestling more generally and are perhaps new to the specific subject matter. These readers will be introduced to a wider world of wrestling, and the book encourages them to explore Japanese wrestling.The third group is a broader group of readers who are not professional wrestling fans. As series such as Vice's *Dark Side of the Ring* demonstrate, the professional wrestling world has produced interesting human stories over the years, involving the lifting of the curtain on an industry so often shrouded in secrecy.

Ganbaru has one such human story at its heart, with core characters affected by the loss of a beloved patriarch and promoter, a power struggle, and a number of tragedies and triumphs along the way. Readers in this third grouping will hopefully enjoy seeing this human drama unfold in all of its unpredictability (and may even find themselves intrigued enough to take a look at the product after reading about its backstory).

Ganbaru is entirely unofficial and is not authorised by All Japan Pro Wrestling, New Japan Pro Wrestling, Pro Wrestling NOAH, or any other wrestling promotion. While the book aims to be as objective as possible, any opinions expressed are mine, unless attributed to others. For readers' assistance in understanding some of the key terms that appear, a glossary is appended after *Ganbaru*'s main narrative.

As noted above, our story focuses on the years 2000 to 2002. However, to truly understand the All Japan split, we must begin earlier. Chapter one starts back in the early 1970s, with another, similar split.

CHAPTER ONE: ORIGINS

To explore All Japan Pro Wrestling's 2000 split, and how the company survived, we must first look at the promotion's place within the Japanese pro wrestling landscape and the esteem in which it was held prior to the events that precipitated the NOAH exodus.

To start from the very beginning, Japanese pro wrestling started in earnest during the post-war period. While there were certainly stories of matches before this time (catch wrestler Matsuda Sokarichi gave fans what was probably the country's first taste with a series of matches in 1887), the sport took off during the post-World War II US occupation.

According to WWE Hall of Famer 'Classy' Freddy Blassie, along with baseball, American troops spread pro wrestling across occupied Japan 'like a bunch of evangelists'[2]. After Joe Louis led a 1951 tour of boxers and wrestlers across the country, a number of retired judo and sumo practitioners decided to train in professional wrestling, with the former sumo standout Rikidōzan among them.

With Japan recovering from the war, professional wrestling gave the country an outlet for its repressed feelings of nationalism. Rikidōzan gave Japanese fans a local hero to cheer for against foreign heels. Unbeknownst to many fans, their Japanese hero originally hailed from Korea. Born Kim Sin-Rak, the future professional wrestling legend was tormented because of his race.

Realising he faced discrimination in Sumo wrestling, he renounced his Korean nationality and changed his name to Mitsuhiro Momota. In Sumo wrestling, Momota was given the *shinoka* (ring name) Rikidōzan. Amassing an impressive record of 135 wins, eighty-two losses, and fifteen draws, Momota reached the rank of *sekiwake*. Believing he still faced a limit to his success due to institutional racism within Sumo wrestling, Rikidōzan left the sport and turned to professional wrestling instead[3].

Some years later, Antonio Inoki appeared on Collision in Korea, a rare professional wrestling event that took place in Pyongyang. He elicited a positive response from an otherwise quiet crowd by claiming Rikidōzan was a North Korean hero who had now finally returned home. This piece of propaganda was misleading, however, as the nation in question did not exist during Rikidōzan's time there. Between his Japanese identity, and later his North Korean one, Rikidōzan's life has been the subject of legendary development.

Regardless of his exact background, however, he undeniably gave Japanese professional wrestling its first major drawcard, someone who managed to get people to leave their houses to watch his matches and then on television, which grew rapidly as a medium during Japan's post-war manufacturing boom. Early on, however, a set was too expensive for the average Japanese household. As a result, people gathered outside to watch Rikidōzan's matches through shop windows. Founded by Rikidōzan in 1951, the Japanese Wrestling Alliance (JWA) was one of the early organisations to ride Japanese pro-wrestling's wave. Televised on both Nippon TV (NTV) and TV Asahi, the promotion was the National Wrestling Alliance's representative in Japan.

From early in its history, Japanese professional wrestling embraced elements of sumo wrestling and integrated these into the core of the western product introduced by touring Americans. In keeping with sumo tradition, upcoming wrestlers lived and trained in a dojo where they were expected to clean up and make *chanko* (a hotpot of vegetables and lots of protein in a chicken broth) for the more experienced wrestlers.

As well as fostering discipline, wrestlers got into the shape that they needed to be in for the rigours of the ring. Trainees also learned legitimate grappling techniques so they knew how to defend themselves should they ever need to, as well as techniques to make their wrestling more believable.

On the other hand, core aspects of the American influence were evident early in Japanese pro wrestling (and remain to this day), including a pinfall, or an out of ring count-out, being counted in English. As well as this, the sport introduced a number of unusual words into the Japanese vernacular, such as 'suplex'.

Following Rikidōzan's death at the hands of a *yakuza* member in 1963, the JWA focused on promoting a new generation of local talent. Two of the company's prominent talents were former Rikidōzan **trainees:** Shohei 'Giant' Baba and Antonio Inoki. Between them, these two wrestlers changed the Japanese wrestling landscape.

With a background in professional baseball, Shohei Baba stood out from his peers, both literally and figuratively. Born with a condition sometimes referred to as giantism, Baba was six foot ten. Training in the JWA dojo under Rikidōzan, Baba no doubt garnered the jealously of his fellow recruits when the company granted him special dispensation to live nearby and commute to training, rather than live in the dojo as was normally required for entry into the promotion[4]. Baba was most likely given this freedom for practical reasons, as his size did not have made for a comfortable stay. Debuting on the same show as Inoki in September 1960, Baba quickly earned fan support. The following year, he undertook a tour of America, where he lived a dual professional existence. In West Coast promotions, he portrayed the babyface 'Big' Shohei Baba, while in New York he was a heel.

In 1971, the JWA's revenue was declining due to what Inoki perceived to be poor decisions, and the young star responded by attempting a hostile takeover. When this failed, Inoki was fired. He eventually formed New Japan Pro Wrestling in March of 1972.

While Baba agreed to stick around after the failed coup, he ultimately opted to not renew his contract. Taking Rikidōzan's sons, Mitsuo and Yoshohiro Momota, with him, Baba formed his own company, All Japan Pro Wrestling. Early in the process of putting the company together, Baba met with NTV executives and put together an arrangement to take the JWA's television deal to this new promotion.

All Japan Pro Wrestling

Shohei Baba promoted All Japan Pro Wrestling's

first card on 21 October 1972. In the main event, he teamed with Thunder Sugiyama against Bruno Sammartino and Terry Funk, losing by count out. Ten months later, the new promotion joined the National Wrestling Alliance (NWA), an alliance of professional wrestling promoters. Membership gave Baba access to talent trades and the ability to book the NWA World Champion on occasion[5]. From the 1970s through to 2000, All Japan Pro Wrestling competed with New Japan Pro Wrestling for the top spot in Japan's professional wrestling industry[6].

In All Japan, Giant Baba could realise his own unique vision for professional wrestling. He ran a promotion where wrestling was treated as a sport. According to wrestling journalist Fumi Saito, Baba ran All Japan like a family business, developing close relationships to some of his key talent. In an interview conducted for this book, Saito said that 'All Japan Pro Wrestling was a big company, but not like WWE corporate. They always kept it that way'.

Reflecting on this corporate culture in his book, *The Last Outlaw*, All Japan mainstay Stan Hansen recalled that, 'When I worked for New Japan, they were run like a true Japanese corporation. Everything was done in the traditional Japanese fashion...[O]ne of the things I noticed when I went to All Japan in 1982 was how lacking in organisation they were compared to New Japan'[7]. While Hansen went on to observe that he never needed to worry about anything other than showing up to wrestle, thanks to the professionalism of the All Japan office, his comparison between the two big Japanese companies supports Saito's description of Baba's operation as a family business.

While All Japan evolved and grew over time, Baba's fingerprints were always over the company, and he ensured that wrestlers adhered to certain traditions. These norms covered everything from how his roster dressed (tights needed to cover the wrestler's navel) to the way that newcomers were trained.

Indeed, Baba insisted that wrestlers learnt how to work in a particular way. In a November 2020 interview with *Slam Wrestling*, former All Japan Pro Wrestling *gaijin* Richard Aslinger described how trainees in the All Japan dojo were required to learn how to shoot (fight) in case they needed these skills, and to protect pro wrestling's image.

He said, 'The Great Kabuki told me that all of us [the AJPW trainees] would get taught how to shoot before we'd take our first bump. That's because kickboxers and other professionals kept coming up to challenge the wrestlers because they thought wrestling is/was fake. The veterans taught us how to shoot so that if those people ever tested us, we could prove them wrong'[8].

Baba's training requirements also carried over to the sound that trainees made when they took a bump in the ring. Until wrestlers learnt how to make this sound, he did not allow them to perform on his shows.

Baba also implemented a dojo system that had a strict hierarchy between the wrestlers and their trainees. Incoming trainees, often those who had excelled at other sports like judo or sumo, were matched up to an experienced wrestler who helped their training. The trainee (*kohei*) often performed menial tasks for their trainer (*senpai*) such as carrying their bags and washing their laundry.

The decision regarding what veteran a young wrestler was paired with often had an impact on their entire career. For example, while Kenta Kobayashi (later KENTA) had key similarities to Toshiaki Kawada and Kenta Kobashi, Misawa found the similarities between the two Kentas' names enough of a coincidence to warrant pairing them. The result was a mentorship that continues today, with KENTA receiving guidance from Kobashi well into his career[9]. Life in the dojo was strict for All Japan's trainees, who, per tradition, were expected to stay on premises and banned from having any kind of nightlife. For these trainees, weekend trips to the *konbibi* (convenience store) were a rare outside break. Moreover, the training itself could be brutal at times, with Stan Hansen going so far to suggest that a court of law may consider it assault[10].

In keeping with another Rikidōzan tradition, Baba placed Japanese faces against foreign heels (bad guys), with a number of famous *gaijin* brought in to play the role of the villain. All Japan flew in wrestlers including Stan Hansen, Bruiser Brody, Terry Funk, his brother Dory Funk Jr, and 'Dr Death' Steve Williams for these tours, and the international talent established themselves in Japan.

All Japan promoted these *gaijin* as being nigh unbeatable. Any match where a Japanese wrestler was able to defeat them was a star-making occasion. For example, Kenta Kobashi lost multiple times to Stan Hansen in their early 90s feud.

Hansen recalled, 'I think Baba, like Rikidōzan, realised that the *gaijins* played an important part in the development of the Japanese wrestlers. There was a period of time where there was great interest in Japanese versus Japanese matches. However, I feel that if the Japanese promotors are honest, they will admit that wrestling and defeating certain *gaijins* was the defining moment which pushed many Japanese wrestlers to a higher level in the eyes of the fans…Misawa, Kawada, Akira Taue, Kobashi, and Jun Akiyama, all fought the top *gaijins* in their bid to get over, and since then, they have all been successful'[11].

According to Fumi Saito, Hansen understood that the appeal of the *gaijin* versus Japanese matchups was that they represented triumph over adversity. Beyond that, having big foreign heels for Japanese faces to feud with represented something outside the typical Japanese person's life experience.

While the traditional *gaijin* versus Japanese matches featured wrestlers from different backgrounds who often spoke different languages, wrestling tradition managed to overcome these differences. According to Hansen and others, the language barrier was not a problem. When a wrestler started working a hold, their opponent's experience and intuition ensured that they could anticipate what was coming next, and how to react[12].

Another tradition that Baba carried out was that his wrestlers needed to adhere to kayfabe, even when they were backstage. A term widely used for how wrestlers carry out the illusion that what they are doing is real, kayfabe is largely intended to preserve audiences' enjoyment of the product. According to Saito, before the advent of internet wrestling sites and the ability to instantly upload information to social media, some journalists and photographers were allowed backstage at wrestling shows with a few restrictions.

During this time, Saito said, he noted that the babyface (good guy) wrestlers had separate locker rooms to the heels (bad guys), and that messages between opponents were carried by busy referees 'Every Korakuen Hall match, I [attended],' he recalled. 'Referees were the only ones going back and forth [between locker rooms].' This, he said, was all in aid of the entertainment of wrestling and 'maintaining your fantasy'.

Much like the language gap between native Japanese wrestlers and their *gaijin* opponents, the gap between locker rooms was something that wrestlers overcame through the referees' notes, and by becoming accustomed to calling the match in the ring. Another facet to *kayfabe* was a distrust of outsiders. Saito said that he was able to befriend some of the wrestlers in this secretive environment, but even then, he was not given unlimited access. 'I knew Stan Hansen very well, but he would never let you in all the way,' he recalled.

Despite Shohei Baba's insistence on certain strictures like kayfabe, wrestlers liked working for him, and he gained a reputation as an honest and fair promoter.

Baba oftentimes opted against contractual agreements with talent, as his word was his bond, and this was evident in the 'handshake deals' he had with his talent. For example, Stan Hansen recalled feeling good after his initial 1981 negotiation with Baba, as he had managed to shake hands with the promoter on a deal. Writing in his book, *The Last*

Outlaw, he explained:

'From what I knew about him, that was worth more than reams of paper. Bruno Sammartino and others had talked about Baba with high regard...Wrestlers were always voicing their opinions on different people, good and bad. Not one time did I hear anyone say anything bad about Baba...not even when I was wrestling for "the other side."

'The one thing I constantly heard about him was that "his word is gold." In other words, we could always count on Baba to keep his promises...I worked for Baba for the next seventeen years, and in those years, long after that original contract expired, we never had another written contract between us. Our future agreements were all done on a handshake'.[13]

During the 1980s and 1990s, All Japan was widely considered to be 'the' place for wrestlers to work due to the low stress environment and time off between tours, as well as how well Baba took care of his talent. During this time, many of the abovementioned foreign wrestlers, such as Stan Hansen, worked all of All Japan's tours, which added up to 26 weeks a year[14]. In addition to this reasonable schedule, Baba paid his talent well. In his first book *Have a Nice Day*, Mick Foley recalls a month-long tour that he did with All Japan in 1991. For his four weeks of work, he was paid $1500 a week, or a total of $6000[15]. At the time of writing, this payoff for

Foley's first tour with the company equalled a little over $12,000. For an independent wrestler on his first-time tour of Japan, this was good, reliable money.

Of course, loyalty to a promotion could not be fostered on money alone, and Baba had a favourable reputation as a fair promoter. In his 2003 book, *Listen, You Pencil Neck Geeks*, WWE Hall of Fame member Classy Freddie Blassie recalled that 'Bruno Sammartino, who never got along with authority figures, said that, if money was ever short, he'd work for All Japan for free'[16].

Touring the country was made all the easier by All Japan providing talent with comfortable accommodation. During the early to mid-1990s, the company booked *gaijin* wrestlers in first class hotels, such as the Tokyu Hotel in Sapporo. At times, this arrangement was a source of consternation among the Japanese wrestlers, who stayed in mid-level business hotels. As Hansen recalled in his book, the arrangement was eventually reversed.

There was some degree of separation between the *gaijin* wrestlers and their Japanese counterparts, with the two booked different hotels and transport, and often changing in separate dressing rooms. Hansen attributed this separation to convenience and a difference in outlook between the two groups, with the *gaijin* locker room often being the louder of the two. It also ensured that the *gaijin* wrestlers were largely left out of the organisation's backstage politics.

While he rarely drank or partied with his talent, Baba provided his talent with all they needed to have a good time. A letter to foreign talents from the 1990s describes how Baba provided them with 'beer for your enjoyment' (but insisted they only partake after their match was finished).

The same fondness that the wrestlers held Shohei Baba in was not extended, however, to Motoko Baba. As we will see, this directly contributed to the All Japan split in 2000. Offering an explanation as to why one was beloved and the other disliked, Hisame writes that Baba was something of an indulgent father figure who kept the boys happy, whereas Motoko was more of a 'strict mother'[17]. *The Wrestling Observer Editor* Dave Meltzer makes this same point using a different analogy, writing that Shohei Baba and Motoko Baba had a 'good cop/bad cop' approach: 'Shohei Baba would be there for the good news. If there was bad news, it came from her, which enabled her husband to maintain a strong and positive reputation to almost everyone, which they both understood was key to his legacy.

As this suggests, Motoko Baba was not simply the 'wife of a promoter' and took an active role in running All Japan. Indeed, she worked together with her husband on every major business decision regarding All Japan. When Giant Baba discussed the business with colleagues, he often said that he had to clear decisions 'with the boss,' meaning Motoko. She also often handled the box office at All Japan shows and worked the merchandise stand, oftentimes with Giant Baba sitting behind her smoking a cigar and signing autographs[18].

Stan Hansen recalled Motoko Baba as being a powerful and integral part of All Japan's operations: 'Mrs Baba always treated me with great respect. She was the "strong woman behind the man" we always hear about. She ran the everyday nuts and bolts of the company so Baba could concentrate on the business of matches and talent. One of her primary jobs was to run Giant Service, the merchandise end of the company. Whenever I negotiated with the company, though, I always dealt with [Shohei] Baba, although I'm sure [Motoko] was privy to what Baba was doing'[19].

Mick Foley recalls that his tour with the promotion did not lead to more after he ran afoul of Motoko Baba when he accidentally injured her favourite wrestler, Johnny Ace. According to Foley, being out of favour with Motoko was not good for a wrestler's career[20].

Despite the antipathy that the 'good cop/bad cop' approach engendered towards Motoko Baba, the relationships that the Babas fostered with their talent sometimes went beyond wrestling. Due to Shohei Baba's reluctance to pass along his giantism to the next generation, the couple opted not to have children. This, it should be noted, was based on the medical advice at the time, and it was not widely known as it is now that the condition is not necessarily genetic.

In any event, without any children of his own, Shohei Baba counted as family a younger cohort of grapplers who worked for him, with the promoter even considering adopting some of them. In a letter Motoko sent Shohei, she wrote that All Japan Pro Wrestling's wrestlers and fans were their children. Some of Baba's trainees who had a mentor-mentee relationship included Tomomi 'Jumbo' Tsuruta, Genichiro Tenryu, Atsushi Onita, Mitsuharu Misawa, and Kenta Kobashi.

The first of these, Tomomi 'Jumbo' Tsuruta, was the inaugural Triple Crown Heavyweight Champion and one half of the first ever 'Double Cup' World Tag Team Champions.

An amateur wrestling standout who won the All Japan Amateur Wrestling Championship in both freestyle and Greco Roman wrestling, Tsuruta was scouted by Baba. He was sent to Texas to train with Dory Funk Jr. With a career that spanned 1973 to 1999, he had 3,329 matches, facing everyone from

Stan Hansen to Ric Flair and Nick Bockwinkel. Tsuruta played a big role in Mitsuharu Misawa's career.

While Tsuruta was initially hesitant and unsuccessfully pushed for a count-out finish, he put the former Tiger Mask over in a big match at the Nippon Budokan. After the bout, the result's meaning was spelled out (in English) by an announcer who yelled, 'New hero!' After Tsuruta's in-ring career was over, he left Japan and moved to the United States to become a visiting university professor in Portland Oregon.

Genichiro Tenryu was another key talent for Baba, and a figure with a key role to play in this book. A former Sumo wrestler who turned to professional wrestling, Tenryu is described by Meltzer as, 'between the fourth and sixth biggest native star' in Japanese wrestling history[21]. As well as being a big drawcard, Tenryu contributed to All Japan's development in a number of ways. He was the second person to win the promotion's Triple Crown Heavyweight Championship. This title match, against inaugural champion Jumbo Tsuruta, was named match of the year by several Japanese magazines.

From there, the trust Baba had for Tenryu was on display when he booked his protégé to pin him in a tag team match, a rare accomplishment. In an event later echoed in 2000, however, Tenryu left All

Japan in April 1990 to form Super World of Sports (SWS), taking other talent with him. Spurned by the defection, Baba swore Tenryu was to never return to All Japan, a declaration that sounded ironic some ten years later.

As well as having an impact on All Japan's talent roster, for good or otherwise, Tenryu's career is closely associated with the above-mentioned Triple Crown Heavyweight Championship, which is the promotion's most prestigious title.

The Triple Crown Heavyweight Championship

Formed in 1989, the Sankan Hebīkyū Ōza, or Triple Crown Heavyweight Championship, is All Japan Pro Wrestling's world title. It amalgamates three prior championships, the PWF World Heavyweight Championship, the former NWA United National Championship, and the former NWA International Championship.

Formed after All Japan left the NWA, the Triple Crown symbolises the promotion's independence and served to provide a single focus point for main events, as Baba ensured title matches always went on last and were treated as events of importance, complete with rituals such as the reading of the title match contract.

During the title's existence, fans and commentators have considered it one of wrestling's most prestigious prizes. The title has also had moments of crisis, however, including during the year 2000 split. Originally represented by all three original belts, All Japan debuted a singular Triple Crown championship belt in 2013, with plates representing each of the original titles.

Of course, the Triple Crown is not the only title in All Japan, as other belts symbolise tag team competition.

The All-Asia Tag Team Championships

The All-Asia Tag Team Championships are some of the oldest professional wrestling titles in the world, dating all the way back to 1955, when they were promoted by the JWA. While the titles were originally vacated in 1973 when that promotion closed, All Japan reactivated them on 26 March 1976. The titles were often used to showcase promising athletes on the promotion's roster, and the list of people who have held the belts read like a who's who of Japanese professional wrestling. The All-Asia Tag Team Championships are considered the 'mid-card' tag team championships after the World Tag Team Championships.

The World Tag Team Championships

Sometimes referred to as the 'Double Cup', the

World Tag Team Championships consist of the former NWA International Tag Team Championships and the PWF World Tag Team Championships, two sets of belts unified on 10 June 1988, when the PWF Champions Jumbo Tsuruta and Yoshiaki Yatsu defeated the NWA International Tag Team Champions The Road Warriors. The titles have been held by some of wrestling's most famous tag teams and are often defended in main event matches.

The World Junior Heavyweight Championship

While All Japan Pro Wrestling is primarily known for its heavyweight wrestlers, the promotion's Junior Heavyweight division has been one of the promotion's cornerstones. Wrestlers under 100 kg (220 pounds) are eligible for the title. It debuted in 1986 to replace the NWA International Junior Heavyweight Championship, when Hiro Saito defeated Brad Armstrong in a tournament final.

While perhaps not as famous as other junior heavyweight championships, such as New Japan Pro Wrestling's renowned IWGP Junior Heavyweight Championship, a number of stars have held the title over the years. Kenny Omega, Maunakea Mossman, Naomichi Marufuji, Último Dragón, and Taka Michinoku are but a few of the champions who have held the title over the years.

Masanobu Fuchi is perhaps the man most associated with the title, however, with a record-setting five reigns. As we will see throughout *Ganbaru*, Fuchi played a key role in post-split All Japan. Having wrestled with All Japan since 1974, he is also its longest-tenured wrestler.

All Japan also gained the All Asia Championship, a mid-card singles title previously active in the JWA and first held by Rikidōzan. The title ran in the promotion from 1976 to 1981. The belt was recently revived in 2017 by Pro Wrestling Land's End, and remains recognised by All Japan's governing body, the Pacific Wrestling Federation (PWF). On 7 October 2012, All Japan established another singles championship, the GAORA TV title. When the promotion was without these two secondary belts, it largely relied on the All Asian Tag Team Championships for mid-card belts to showcase their roster.

In order to set up future bouts and signal which wrestlers contended for these belts (or in some cases who held them), All Japan hold a variety of tournaments. These events allow the promotion an avenue for their long-term booking decisions and give fans a regular set of dates they can look forward to each year.

The Champion Carnival

All Japan Pro Wrestling's biggest annual tournament is the *Chanpion Kānibaru* or Champion Carnival. The event is similar to the JWA's World League tournament (and later, New Japan Pro Wrestling's G1 Climax). The Carnival dates back to 1973, although it did not run during the years from 1983 to 1990. The tournament has been held across a variety of formats over the years, but is generally a round robin, with participants scoring points for a win.

More often than not, The Champion Carnival has taken place across two blocks, with the wrestlers with the most point in each meeting in the final. The winner of the Champion Carnival gains the opportunity to wrestle for the Triple Crown Heavyweight Championship, unless the champion himself enters the tournament and wins. In that event, the Triple Crown Champion will, per storyline terms, 'choose' his next challenger.

The tournament is also known by the nickname *Haru no Saiten*, or Spring Festival, as it generally takes place in April. All Japan often invites outsiders from outside the promotion to participate, which adds to the event's popularity and unpredictability. A similar round robin tournament with this practice is the World's Strongest Tag Determination

League.

World's Strongest Tag Determination League

Similarly to the Champion Carnival, the *Sekai Saikyō Taggu Kettei Rīgu-sen,* or World's Strongest Tag Determination League, is an annual round robin tournament. The tournament has run since 1977, when Dory Funk Jr and Terry Funk won the inaugural event. Much like the Carnival, the event sometimes uses blocks, but has also been a single block round robin, with tag teams earning points for wins or draws.

Between 1988 and 1994, the World Tag Team Champions annually vacated their belts for the tournament, with the winning team receiving the titles. More recent tournaments have tended to award the number one contendership as the prize. The World's Strongest Tag League is generally the last tournament of the year, beginning in November or December.

While the event is sometimes referred to in the West as the Real World Tag League, this is something of a mistranslation of *Saikyō*, which is better translated as 'strong' than 'real'[22]. The use of 'Real' may, however, be distinguish the tournament from New Japan Pro Wrestling's World Tag League, which also traditionally takes place at the end of the year. Of course, the names of the promotions' respective tournaments are not all that distinguish All Japan from New Japan, and there are stylistic points worth considering when looking at the former's history.

The King's Road Style

Over time, Giant Baba oversaw the development of All Japan Pro Wrestling's unique '*Oudou*' or 'King's Road' wrestling style, while New Japan Pro Wrestling promoted itself as featuring 'Strong Style'. While both of these wrestling styles emphasised physicality and 'fighting spirit' there were certainly differences between them that made for altogether different bouts.

King's Road blended a traditional technical grappling style with a uniquely Japanese approach emphasising 'fighting spirit' and engaging the audience with emotional storytelling. After many big matches in the 1970s and 1980s ending via count out or disqualification, Baba was determined to ensure some definitive wins, and so King's Road matches ended with clear cut winners.

In promoting the *Oudou* style, Baba coined the description, 'bright, fun, tough, new'[23]. Wrestlers engaged in an all-out battle for victory, never giving up, despite taking some immense bumps and. sometimes, legitimately stiff strikes. In exhilarating and legitimately dangerous matches, they targeted one another's heads and necks in a constant game of one-upmanship[24].

While undeniably violent, King's Road was not a mindless style by any stretch, and the matches blended danger with long-form storytelling, psychology, and references to previous matches. For example, during the 1995 Champion Carnival tournament, Mitsuharu Misawa broke his orbital bone in an early exchange with Toshiaki Kawada. After a match that looked even nastier, Misawa gutted it out to make the tournament final against Akira Taue. As part of this match's psychology, Taue focused his attacks on Misawa's face, drawing intense crowd heat in the form of continual booing.

While Taue's eye-raking seemed the act of a desperate heel, this tactic served to get across just how willing he was to defeat the more established Misawa. This in-ring storytelling was aided by the coverage of professional wrestling in publications like *Tokyo Sports* and *Weekly Pro Wrestling*, which informed the audience on a regular basis, ensuring they reacted to some of the product's subtleties. King's Road matches were therefore layered and well-booked, with moments that dated back to prior shows.

Richard Aslinger described wrestling the King's Road style as being akin to painting a portrait. 'It's the only style of pro wrestling I know. It's all about being snug, believable, and credible,' said Aslinger (who wrestled as Richard Slinger).

He also said, 'That era was one of a kind. I don't think it can ever be recreated'[25].

Aslinger cited an in-ring exchange with Kenta Kobashi as an example of what it was like to be in the ring during this era. '[Kobashi] caught one of my kicks and hit the Burning Lariat. He landed it so hard it busted my lip, and I needed stitches. I was out. Then I felt something tugging on me. It was Kobashi, and he wanted to hit it again because he didn't think it looked good. That left the fans asking themselves, "Was it a work? Was it a shoot?"'[26]

More than simply being hard hitting or believable, King's Road stood out as a technique unique to All Japan. Baba honed this style so as to distinguish All Japan from its competitors.

With 'shoot style' promotions offering a more pure sporting presentation, and MMA on the rise in Japan, Baba saw that a professional wrestling product could draw with decisive finishes and an emphasis on believable in-ring action. As Chris Charlton writes, 'disqualifications were stripped out as was, for the most part, interference or other clichéd illegal acts. Instead, the fat was trimmed away from an earnest in ring presentation'.

In order to further distinguish All Japan from its competitors, King's Road also eschewed the submission finishes that Inoki's New Japan Pro Wrestling had embraced as part of its Strong Style. Instead, King's Road placed its emphasis squarely on the final elusive pinfall. In 2011, Toshiaki Kawada recalled that 'Baba loathed submissions. One, two, three was the rule, especially in Triple Crown matches...[E]ach match was about breaking the limit you set in your last'[27].

All of this, however, took a toll on participants. As injuries piled up, 1990s All Japan became something of a cautionary tale for wrestling promotions (Meltzer, 2018). As we will see throughout *Ganbaru*, this included some serious injuries for the promotion's big stars.

As with all wrestling matches, the referee was the third 'participant' in the Triple Crown Heavyweight Title bouts. All Japan Pro Wrestling's Kyohei Wada is a veteran official so well known that he often receives an ovation from fans, who cheer his name when it is mentioned at the start of a match[28].

Wada was quite literally at the centre of a number of these classics. He said that Baba encouraged the competitors to do whatever they needed to in order to stand out: 'Baba told the younger talent "Whatever you want to do, do it, and whatever you want to show the people, show it." He said that if one move didn't get you a three count, it made no sense to do the same thing and expect different results. So, King's Road was about escalating to a crescendo. Refereeing these matches was like conducting a symphony'[29].

The King's Road style proved to be influential for wrestlers all around the world, who saw the matches and sought to emulate the style in their own work. Kenny Omega, who was a star in New Japan Pro Wrestling and a former IWGP Heavyweight Champion, referred to this influence in a 2017 interview.

'Kawada, Kobashi, Misawa, Akiyama, Stan Hansen, those dudes were bringing forward a style that really couldn't be reproduced anywhere, and you really had to watch it in All Japan or you wouldn't see it anywhere else,' Omega said.

Due to this unique style, All Japan Pro Wrestling also managed to create a unique buzz in Japan and abroad, hitting a financial and critical peak in the mid-1990s.

Shortly after Misawa headlined the 8 June 1990 show at the Nippon Budokan, All Japan sold out all tickets for around 200 consecutive shows at the venue until early 1996, an unreachable record that, as wrestling journalist and historian Dave Meltzer writes, 'Almost surely...has never been approached by any company in any major city in the history of the business'[30]. The closest equivalent in American wrestling is probably Bruno Sammartino's 45 consecutive sell-outs of Madison Square Garden[31].

According to Stan Hansen, All Japan recognised and celebrated this success in a unique way: 'At the 35th straight sell-out, the wrestling office gave every wrestler on the shows a metal pin-on button and continued the practice for every sell-out (more than 100) during that run. They also had a Japanese tradition of paying 1,000 Yen ($10) for a sold-out show. It wasn't much, but it was the thought of as giving something to us for being a part of the sold-out show. The office even explained beforehand that it would only be a token amount'[32].

While selling out the Budokan, All Japan made the arena synonymous with the promotion's big shows. While other promotions occasionally booked the venue, Baba's company was the one most associated with it, booking around eight dates a year in the building, promoting these as being significant events.

The earlier-mentioned trend of Japan becoming a trendsetter for the rest of the world continued with the promotion's domestic success.

As western fans in the 1990s' nascent tape-trading scene clamoured for something new and different to what they could find from American wrestling, All Japan churned out classic match after classic match, and won the *Wrestling Observer Newsletter*'s award for Promotion of the Year in 1990, 1991, and 1993. Baba himself won the newsletter's award for Promoter of the Year every year from 1990 to 1994.

In addition to awards, All Japan was recognised in the deference that American wrestlers paid to the promotion, including when it came to liberally 'borrowing' moves and spots from the promotion's famous wrestlers and matches. As Kenny Omega put it: 'You really know you've made an impact on wrestling history when people from across the globe, from that point on and for years to come, are trying to copy that style, are trying to take that style and make it their own — or just shamelessly rip it off'[33].

The hype that King's Road generated was felt internationally—and wrestlers were attempting to replicate it. The US indy scene in particular saw the proliferation of wrestlers who tried to ape what they saw in wrestling tapes, copying some of the moves that they saw in All Japan, 'without any understanding of the narrative context of these moves'[34]. While this arguably had a negative effect on the US scene in those cases where wrestlers could not adequately replicate the King's Road style, it showed the growth that All Japan was experiencing.

This influence was not limited to wrestlers' move sets and carried over to in-ring attire as well. As

Fumi Saito observed, 'People like Seth Rollins, Kevin Owens, and Chris Jericho don't even kick but they wear the kick pads. They dress like Japanese wrestlers'.

Mitsuharu Misawa, Kenta Kobashi, Toshiaki Kawada, and Akira Taue were four of the key wrestlers leading the way. In many ways, mid-1990s All Japan was built on these four men, and they were largely responsible for the critical acclaim that All Japan received, especially after Tenryu's dramatic exit. With the promotion's roster depleted by the SWS exodus, necessity bred innovation as the promotion encouraged these four to create a new vision of professional wrestling. Embodying the King's Road style, Misawa, Kobashi, Kawada, and Taue became the four wrestlers who carried the promotion throughout the 1990s.

The Four Pillars of Heaven

When Genichiro Tenryu left All Japan, Baba turned to Misawa, Kobashi, Kawada, and Taue: four talented younger wrestlers. Eventually, All Japan was built around these four, who had some of the best matches of all time against one another in singles and tag team matches.

Baba attached the term *Puroresu Shi Tennou*,[35] to this group. It should be noted that, while commonly referred to as 'The Four Pillars of Heaven', this term may be mistranslated in English. Long-term wrestling journalist Fumi Saito is among those who contend that there are options for a better translation of the term[36]. In an interview conducted for this book, he elaborated: 'That Four Pillars name is another example of mistranslation or something lost in translation. *Shi tennou* is actually a Buddhist term. *Shi* is four and *Tennou* is diva/deity/deities. So the *Shi tennou* is The Four Divas or simply The Big Four. I don't know where this pillar thing came from. It's not a wrestling word, but often used in sports. The Four Divas/deity, deities, or simply The Big Four'.

The term, then, comes from Buddhist imagery, namely four beings that are represented in statues in holy places such as temples or crematoriums. By referring to Misawa, Kobashi, Kawada, and Taue along these lines, Baba was making the point that they were protecting All Japan in the post-Tenryu era. Author and New Japan Pro Wrestling English commentator Chris Charlton agrees with Saito that the translated terms 'four pillars' is therefore not literally correct when applied to All Japan's core four wrestlers.

He pointed out, however, that he doesn't take issue with it: 'I don't have a massive issue with the pillars term per se. 四天王 literally means four heavenly kings, referring to four deities looking over the land, and it's a concept that gets extended to all forms of media from anime to games and the original プロレス四天王。While it's definite that pillars doesn't sound as grand, and is literally incorrect, it conveys who they are as cornerstones of a business, the four last bosses so to speak, especially when expressing the concept outside of a polytheistic mind set'.

Mitsuharu Misawa became All Japan Pro Wrestling's ace and a multiple Triple Crown champion. In many ways, he is a central figure to this book, and to All Japan's lore in general. Misawa's early upbringing was violent. Born to a father who was physically abusive towards his wife, a young Misawa wanted to learn how to defend himself. He gravitated towards the escapism offered by pro wrestling[37]. After his parents divorced, Misawa cut all ties to his father. He later had Baba stand in at the parts of his wedding where a father's presence was needed.

During his high school years, Misawa left home and lived in a dormitory. Misawa's roommate and close friend at the time was a boy one year younger than him, Toshiaki Kawada, who went on to play an even bigger role in his life during his professional wrestling career.

During his first major role in the promotion, Misawa became Tiger Mask II. After Baba obtained the licence for the Tiger Mask gimmick, he reportedly handed it to Misawa with a gruff 'wear this'[38].

Misawa enjoyed working as a junior heavyweight, featuring in high profile matches such as a bout against Bret Hart at the Tokyo Dome. The gimmick ran its course, however. On 14 May, during a tag match, Misawa surprised the crowd when he asked tag team partner Toshiaki Kawada to help him to unmask.

Shortly afterwards, Misawa gained a signature win over Jumbo Tsuruta at the Budokan on 8 June 1990. The result was far from certain, with Tsuruta initially reluctant to lose, requesting to Baba to lose via count out. With his petition denied, Tsuruta went on to put Misawa over in grand fashion, with a classic match that ended with Misawa emerging victorious after a close competition over the final, decisive pinfall.

The result turned out to be the right one for Misawa and All Japan Pro Wrestling's bottom line, based on sheer fan reaction. Fumi Saito recalled that audience members were crying after witnessing the result.

Misawa spent much of the 1990s engaged in multiple matches against Kobashi, Kawada, and Taue, garnering multiple match of the year nominations. His performances stand out among his peers.

Misawa holds the record for five star matches according to Dave Meltzer, with twenty-five such reviews. Beyond any number of highly rated matches, Misawa's legacy extends to countless wrestlers whose careers he inspired, with contemporary examples including Go Shiozaki and Kaito Kiyomiya[39].

Misawa's contributions to All Japan Pro Wrestling were not confined to the squared circle. In 1997, he became All Japan's booker, deciding on finishes and storyline direction, after Shohei Baba handed him this responsibility with the simple instruction, 'You—do it!'[40]. In 1999, Misawa became the company's president. The circumstances behind this promotion were far from happy, however. Misawa's ascendency occurred because Giant Baba passed away in 1999. While Motoko Baba had wanted to make the elder Mitsuo Momota president, the majority of All Japan's locker room viewed Misawa as a leader. Tensions over these arrangements eventually led to the 2000 split.

Next, we will explore Misawa's tag partner and later rival Kenta Kobashi. A standout in judo and rugby, Kobashi trained in All Japan Pro Wrestling's dojo, debuting in 1988. During his time as a young wrestler, Kobashi went on a long losing streak, winning over wrestling fans with his underdog efforts and 'fighting spirit'. Kobashi holds twenty-three five star matches according to Meltzer due to his penchant for dramatic and physical matches. He put himself through a tough training regime to prepare for the ring, which included practicing lariats on metal poles and chops on concrete walls[41].

Kobashi was widely praised for his toughness, with Stan Hansen singling him out as one of his favourite opponents for this reason. 'Whenever we wrestled, I knew he was going to be stiff from start to finish, and he never complained when I potatoed him,' Hansen wrote. 'As the saying goes, he was as tough as a boot'[42].

Kobashi was not only tough, but also mastered the art of long-term storytelling in his matches. During his long-running feud against Misawa, Kobashi appeared to be unable to put his opponent away, coming up short in every match until the 2000 Champion Carnival. This rivalry ran from the early 1990s all the way up until their final match on 1 March 2003.

Toshiaki Kawada holds a unique position in All Japan Pro Wrestling lore. As indicated, it is impossible to separate Kawada's career from that of Misawa, with their association dating all the way back to their high school days. The two established a friendship that was similar to brotherhood.

Kawada is widely known as one of the toughest professional wrestlers in history, a reputation built on his ability to fight through injuries to deliver quality, physical matches. Perhaps the most famous example comes from a Triple Crown match Kawada had against Misawa on 22 January 1999. Around seven minutes into the match, Kawada hit Misawa with an errant spinning backfist, breaking both his forearm and his wrist.

Despite what must have been excruciating pain, Kawada fought on for well over twenty minutes, lasting through to the match's planned finish. The bout ended with Kawada pinning Misawa to claim the Triple Crown, but he later vacated the belts due to his injury.

As well as his ability to absorb pain, Kawada is also known for the physicality of his style. Teaming with Akira Taue, Kawada was half of the acclaimed Holy Demon Army tag team, winning the World Tag Team Championship from Misawa and Kobashi in a match that *Tokyo Sports* named as its match of the year for 1995.

Kawada was one of two members of the All Japan permanent native roster who did not leave for Pro Wrestling NOAH, a decision that allowed 'Dangerous K' to carve out his own unique legacy. At the time of writing, Kawada still holds the record for the most defences of the Triple Crown Heavyweight Championship, at ten. His 529-day reign lasted from 6 September 2003 to 16 February 2005 and helped stabilise the Triple Crown as a prestigious title after a tumultuous period.

While perhaps not as famous as the others, Akira

Taue is widely regarded as one of the most innovative wrestlers ever, with fourteen five star matches according to the *Wrestling Observer*. Taue was a Sumo wrestling standout who began his professional wrestling career as a trainee in Ricki Choshu's breakaway promotion, JPW.

When JPW's wrestlers joined All Japan as part of a long invasion angle, Taue transferred to the promotion's dojo. He went on to have an illustrious career, recognised as having a unique creativity when it came to how he laid out his matches and the moves that he invented, such as the *Ore ga Taue*, a belly-to-back chokeslam.

Taue is a multiple world champion, having won the Triple Crown Heavyweight Championship and GHC Heavyweight Championship in Pro Wrestling NOAH. Taue also won the World Tag Team Championship multiple times during his All Japan run, with six of these taking place as one half of the Holy Demon Army.

Although not a part of the Four Pillars, Jun Akiyama is a wrestler whose career was very close to theirs. Akiyama had many great matches with Misawa, Kobashi, Kawada, and Taue. He also holds a unique place in All Japan history as the last dojo graduate to be directly trained by Shohei 'Giant' Baba[43]. Akiyama had major matches in All Japan, including when he defeated Mitsuharu Misawa on 27 February 2000 in an acclaimed contest.

All Japan was garnering buzz thanks to its competitors' efforts and appeared to be leveraging this to make money through merchandising opportunities. The company licenced its wrestlers' likenesses for action figures and videogames, and sold video tapes (and, later, DVDs) of its shows.

One key piece of merchandise was the popular Nintendo 64 game *Virtual Pro Wrestling 2: Ōdō Keishō* (Royal Road Succession). While the game initially received fair to mediocre reviews (scoring thirty out of forty in the Japanese magazine *Famitsu* and 7.9 out of ten in an IGN import review)[44], it has since garnered a much better reputation and sold well. It was an especially favoured import title among Western fans, becoming the second-most imported Nintendo 64 title after *Sin and Punishment*.

Such revenue streams appeared to set the company up, but certain arrangements saw to it that All Japan relied mainly on ticket revenue. These financial decisions were one of several factors that led directly to the 2000 split.

Conclusion to Chapter One

Two decades into the promotion's existence, All Japan Pro Wrestling was enjoying a unique place atop the wrestling world. The mid-1990s was marked by unprecedented financial and critical success, led by the quartet of Misawa, Kobashi, Kawada, and Taue. Indeed, All Japan's mix of drama, athleticism, and unique King's Road style led to a record-breaking run for the company, allowing it to overtake its main rival, Antonio Inoki's New Japan Pro Wrestling. We will now examine this rivalry, as *Ganbaru*'s second chapter considers the relationships between All Japan and its competitors.

CHAPTER TWO: ALL JAPAN PRO WRESTLING AND OTHER PROMOTIONS

During the 1990s, All Japan Pro Wrestling was a vaunted, hot professional wrestling product, revered in the eyes of Japanese and Western fans. The promotion largely achieved this within the confines of the 'walled garden', as Giant Baba opted to not rely on other Japanese promotions and their talents, instead developing and showcasing his own talent using their own signature style. While there were some exceptions, this approach saw All Japan become a force unto itself, operating on its own until after the year 2000 split.

New Japan Pro Wrestling and All Japan Pro Wrestling both started during the same calendar year, after their founders, Antonio Inoki and Shohei 'Giant' Baba respectively, left the JWA to strike out on their own. With New Japan holding its first show in March of 1972, and All Japan following later in October, the stage was set for a rivalry that lasted for decades. There were certainly other players: Isao Yoshiwara's International Wrestling Enterprise (IWE) and Tokyo Pro Wrestling were two contemporaries that gathered crowds and booked some major international talent. For its part, the JWA did not die out immediately after the talent exodus, lasting another year. However, despite these companies, and their contributions to Japan's wrestling history, the main rivalry was clearly between All Japan and New Japan.

The relationship between the competitors had its ups and downs. According to some of the talent working for All Japan, the late 1970s and early 1980s saw moments of antipathy. Talent was one of the issues that caused animosity. After New Japan poached Abdullah the Butcher, All Japan retaliated. Stan Hansen shocked the wrestling world when he showed up at an All Japan show.

In the foreword to Hansen's biography, *The Last Outlaw*, the usually kindly wrestling legend Terry Funk describes the visceral hatred that All Japan's *gaijins* developed for New Japan after Hansen jumped ship from Inoki's promotion to join Baba's: 'We hated New Japan. If Baba asked us to go to one of Inoki's shows and kick the shit out of their guys, we would have done just that. Inoki would have done the same to us if he had been given the opportunity. I hated the opposition...and so did Stan Hansen. He didn't want to just draw a bigger crowd than Inoki. He wanted to bury them, and I did, too. That's the only way you can have a war. Did I talk to their guys? No! Did Stan? No! We were pissed if we didn't outperform their guys. It was a matter of pride and Stan had that pride'[45].

As Funk suggests, there was an inter-company 'war' between the two promotions vying for the top of Japan's wrestling industry. All Japan and New Japan often competed with one another by booking televised events and house shows on the same date, with both promoters (Baba and Inoki) working as star attractions against well-paid monster heels[46]. As odd as it may sound, this competition extended to the warring promotions' respective fandoms who were fiercely loyal to their chosen promotion.

As the war continued, New Japan Pro Wrestling managed to garner momentum, and by the 1980s, Inoki's promotion had overtaken Baba's in terms of ratings and ticket sales. New Japan's stacked roster and 'Strong Style' appealed to Japan's wrestling fans, and Antonio Inoki's fame played a large role in the company taking the number one spot at the box office and in TV ratings.

Aware that his company had been eclipsed, Baba

opted to not run the Champion Carnival from 1983 to 1990, as Baba wanted to avoid competition from New Japan's summertime tournament, now known as the G1 Climax[47].

At other points, however, All Japan was more aggressive in its approach. During the 1980s, All Japan's television broadcast partner NTV became more involved in the company. With his company running in the red, Baba reached out to NTV for help. The broadcast company responded by transferring NTV executive Mitsuo Mitsune in as All Japan's new president. This allowed Baba to transfer All Japan's debts to NTV at a time when other companies that he owned were performing well. Under Mitsune, All Japan aggressively pursued talent, signing prominent *gaijin* talents away from New Japan. Relations further soured between the two rival *puroresu* companies.

In 1984, the New Japan faction formerly known as *Ishin Gundan* (Revolutionary Army) formed their own organisation, Japan Pro Wrestling (JPW). With Mitsune willing to spend money on bringing defectors in, it was a matter of time before All Japan capitalised on this shift in the wrestling landscape. After a few independent shows, JPW 'invaded' All Japan in 1985, leading to a banner year for the promotion, with a number of classic bouts resulting from their battles with the company.

Decades before the New World Order angle drew

American wrestling fans in with the hook of a pseudo-invasion of WCW by the WWF, the promotion tantalised *puroresu* fans with the prospect of seeing a group of New Japan talent leading an incursion into their biggest competitor. The JPW invasion angle, and resulting matches, led to critical and financial success for All Japan.

As with many such storylines, the invasion angle ultimately had a limited shelf-life and on 23 March 1987, core members of the JPW left and eventually re-joined New Japan. In later interviews, Ricki Choshu claimed that the *Ishin Gundan* 'invasion' was the brainchild of Antonio Inoki. According to Choshu, the New Japan founder was keen to demonstrate his promotion's stars were superior draws, including when they worked elsewhere[48]. Not all of the talent returned to Inoki, however, with the likes of Haruka Eigen and Yoshiaki Yatsu staying with All Japan.

Perhaps the biggest contribution from the JPW remnants came from a trainee who had never wrestled on any of the promotion's shows. Akira Taue transferred to All Japan's Dojo and made a career for himself in the promotion, eventually being one of the company's Four Pillars.

Unlike Akira Taue, Mitsuo Mitsune did not last with All Japan. NTV eventually became concerned at the way All Japan's ambitious president burnt through money during the battle for talent. NTV removed

Mitsune in 1989 and returned Baba to running the company that he started[49].

While 1990s All Japan Pro Wrestling largely relied on the concept of a 'walled garden', the company's rich history is full of examples of what they could achieve working with their international partners. All Japan's early membership of the National Wrestling Alliance (NWA) meant that All Japan recognised the NWA World Heavyweight Championship and could book the champion on occasion.

While the NWA affiliation was important to All Japan, it did not prevent Baba from also working with the American Wrestling Association (AWA). For All Japan's thirteenth anniversary show in October 1985, Baba booked NWA World Champion Ric Flair against AWA World Champion Rick Martel. Despite the thorny politics involved, he arranged for the match to be for both titles, with an indecisive finish meaning that both men retained their belts[50]. In 1988, All Japan withdrew from the NWA, creating the Triple Crown Heavyweight Championship the next year as its own world championship.

Despite the 1990s 'walled garden' era, All Japan also sometimes cooperated with other Japanese promotions, for mutual benefit. On 26 August 1979, All Japan and New Japan talent appeared together on a super card at the Nippon Budokan promoted by

Tokyo Sports. The card saw Baba and Inoki reunite their old B-I Cannon tag team, defeating Abdullah the Butcher and Tiger Jeet Singh in the main event.

Over a decade later, another exceptional show took place. When New Japan Pro Wrestling needed to make hasty line-up changes to a Tokyo Dome show on 10 February 1990, Baba agreed to send some talent under the condition they did not lose or be made to look bad during the show. The show saw New Japan talent joined by Steve Williams, Jumbo Tsuruta, Yoshiaki Yatsu, Genichiro Tenryu, Mitsuharu Misawa (under the Tiger Mask gimmick), Stan Hansen, and Larry Zybszko (due to All Japan's working relationship with the AWA)[51].

While cooperation was something of a theme, wrestlers still felt the tensions of competition, and this was especially evident during a match between Stan Hansen and Vader. As Hansen wrote in his book, 'I'm sure neither he nor New Japan wanted him to look [weak]...Of course to a certain extent, I was thinking the same thing, only from my viewpoint. After all, we were in Japan, and I was representing All Japan'[52].

With neither competitor wanting to look bad on behalf of their home promotion, the match was a stiff display, both men hitting the other as hard as they could. Despite Hansen's vision being terrible without his glasses, the Texan brawler damaged Vader far more than he expected to, knocking his eye out of its socket during the melee. After Vader put the eye back into its socket, the two resumed their match, brawling outside the ring. The bout ended in a politically necessitated double count out, a finish that kept both looking strong and was in keeping with Baba's conditions.

Despite the horrendous injury to Vader, the physical nature of the brawl, and the competition between the two companies, Stan Hansen said there were no hard feelings between him and Vader: 'I wasn't sure what to expect from Leon when I got back to the dressing room. As I waited for him to come back, it crossed my mind that he might try and go at it again in the dressing room because of what I had done to his eye.

'He came into my dressing room and said, "Great match, man." I was relieved that he wasn't pissed off. I'm sorry it happened like it did, but I didn't intentionally injure his eye. Things like that occasionally happen in the ring...Years later he told me he has permanent damage to his eye, with the eye being moved off centre. I don't think the term "fake" pertains to our wrestling'[53].

The show proved to be successful at the box office, with Dave Meltzer summarising it thus: '[New Japan] asked for help and Baba stepped up. It was for the best in the end since they sold the building out'[54]. A decade later, the roles were reversed, with

All Japan reaching out to New Japan to help fill their cards.

On 2 April 1995 (the same night as Wrestlemania 11), All Japan joined twelve other promotions in a Tokyo Dome show promoted by Baseball Magazine Sha (who produce the magazine *Weekly Pro Wrestling*). Unofficially known as 'Bridge of Dreams', the show featured most major Japanese wrestling promotions, with the exception of Genichiro Tenryu's WAR, which had an existing booking nearby at Korakuen Hall.

Fumi Saito, who worked for *Weekly Pro Wrestling* at the time, recalled that getting Baba to agree to the show had been difficult. Part of the issue was that the show was scheduled to take place two weeks before Baba's promotion ran in the Budokan. 'That was so hard [to put together] …I have a gut feeling they had to pay Baba more,' Saito said.

'[Magazine publisher] Tarzan Yamamoto did all the negotiation. Actually, Giant Baba's All Japan was the last company that wanted to do it. Baba was so hard to deal with. [He was asking,] "We'll be having a Budokan Show two weeks after that. Is that going to interfere with our Budokan show?" Their 15 April Budokan show was sold out too. Wrestling was still big in the 1990s.'

Each company was paid a fee and instructed to bring their best match. Choosing the line-up proved to be another political consideration, with the promoters supposedly determining the match order via the order of when the company was founded, the newer companies going on first. This, however, was somewhat misleading, as All Japan Women's Pro Wrestling (a company unrelated to All Japan Pro Wrestling) formed in 1968, yet was booked on the undercard[55].

Despite Baba's initial reluctance, All Japan provided the Tokyo Dome card with its semi-main event, a six-man tag team match featuring the Champion Carnival competitors still eligible to win the tournament. Akira Taue, Johnny Ace, and Toshiaki Kawada faced off against Kenta Kobashi, Stan Hansen, and Mitsuharu Misawa. Fuelled by the competitive desire to demonstrate their product's superiority, the competitors delivered what could arguably be deemed the best match of the show. For thirty minutes, each participant showed no signs of trying to preserve themselves for an ongoing tournament, and the match ended in a time limit draw.

Baba was less willing to work with other promotions during the 1990s, but there were a few exceptions. When Baba became a fan of the FMW wrestler Hayabusa, he agreed to work a little with the smaller promotion, booking Hayabusa in the 1997 World's Strongest Tag Determination League.

A history of defections

In a society where workplace promotions are based on seniority, and where many employees remain with the one company for the duration of their careers, Japan's professional wrestling scene stresses loyalty to wrestlers' home promotion. Wrestlers oftentimes train in a company's dojo and remain loyal from that point on.

Paradoxically, however, *puroresu* history is littered with promotions formed by breaking away from others. This description extends to All Japan itself. A number of promotions formed this way as wrestlers left Baba's employ to strike out on their own.

Perhaps the most acrimonious split during Shohei Baba's lifetime took place when Genichiro Tenryu led the infamous exodus to form Super World of Sports (SWS). Tenryu's departure from All Japan appeared amicable enough. After feeling for a long time he was not being appreciated, or becoming the star he could be, he approached Baba in April 1990. Baba and Tenryu had a long conversation. In the end, Baba apparently gave his blessing to the departure, saying 'If your mind's made up, there's nothing I can do to stop you'[56]. Quickly recruited by Megane Super boss Hachiro Tanaka for the company's ambitious foray into professional wrestling, Tenryu used his popularity in the All Japan Pro Wrestling locker room to recruit a wave of talent and staff from his former company.

Baba responded with his now-infamous claim Tenryu would never return to All Japan. The relationship between the two companies was an adversarial one, in which Baba had the support of then-*Weekly Pro Wrestling* editor, Takarshi 'Tarzan' Yamamoto.

In the pages of his editorials, Yamamoto labelled the SWS, 'a black ship' and 'Sell Out Pro Wrestling.' He also accused Tenryu of being a mercenary who could be bought and paid for. Later, Yamamoto explained his rationale for the commentary: 'New Japan had the funds to prevent Mutoh from leaving [for the SWS],' he wrote. 'AJPW didn't have that protection. I decided to side with Baba'[57].

Initially, SWS showed promise. The new promotion aimed to combine a wide range of professional wrestling styles, united under a hard-hitting philosophy and the tagline 'Straight and Strong'. After WWF's plans to buy out a Japanese promotion saw both New Japan and All Japan distance themselves from the American business leader, the ambitious new SWS formed a working relationship with the McMahons.

The main fruits of this venture were a number of joint shows, including two at the Tokyo Dome. While the shows boasted strong attendance, the

SWS was a money drain, and before too long, Tenryu found himself in the uncomfortable position of needing to release talent.

'[Tanaka would] tell me "we have to restructure," and leave me to fire these guys,' Tenryu said later. 'Those guys would get the news from me, and then go on to Tanaka's office, where he'd pep talk them and say "all the best." So, I'm looking like the bad guy'[58]. Tenryu resigned from his front office role with the SWS on 14 May 1992. The company subsequently cancelled its May shows, folding shortly after its final card on 19 June 1992. As Fumi Saito summarised it, 'SWS was a bitter experience [for Tenryu]'. He would rebound, however, later forming his own promotion called Wrestle and Romance (WAR).

Atsushi Onita was another person who left All Japan to form his own company, FMW. Onita trained in the All Japan dojo. After an excursion to the United States, he returned to Japan as a hot prospect, becoming the World Junior Heavyweight Champion. When he badly injured his leg in a match, however, Onita's athletic prospects were curtailed. Unable to wrestle as a high-flyer, he instead turned to other ways of getting by, becoming a hardcore wrestler who used everyday items as in-ring weapons. Onita split from All Japan to form Frontier Martial Arts Wrestling (FMW)[59]. Onita's exit was particularly shocking for Baba, as the two had a close relationship. Baba considered adopting Onita, who was something of a son to him. His move out of All Japan described as him 'running away from home'[60].

Another departure saw the Great Kojika leave All Japan in 1986. He went on to form his own company, *Dai Nippon Puroresu* or Big Japan Pro Wrestling in 1995, a promotion that combines 'death match' wrestling with traditional matches.

The company has seen its share of highs and lows over the years, but it has remained a constant in Japanese pro wrestling. Big Japan has since worked with All Japan, sharing talent for key shows and tournaments.

Puroresuringuzerowan, or Pro Wrestling Zero One, is another company relevant to *Ganbaru*'s narrative. While Shinya Hashimoto formed the company by breaking away from New Japan rather than All Japan, Zero One later partnered with All Japan, and continues to cooperate with the promotion at the time of writing.

Conclusion to Chapter Two

All Japan generally operated as an island unto itself, but on a few occasions opted to cooperate with other promotions as business imperatives dictated. Where Chapter Two looked mainly at intense interpromotional feuds, Chapter Three will look inwards, examining some of the dynamics within All Japan and the way one rivalry in particular threatened the company's very existence.

CHAPTER THREE: RUPTURES IN ALL JAPAN

All Japan Pro Wrestling enjoyed something of a boom period in the mid-1990s, garnering a number of five star matches and starting a new record for the number of sold-out shows they held in Tokyo. The company managed to edge out its traditional rival, New Japan Pro Wrestling on several occasions, an ongoing competition that looked set to play out for decades to come. This success was not to last, however, as *puroresu*'s overall popularity took a nose-dive.

Tensions between All Japan's new company president Mitsuharu Misawa and company owner Motoko Baba continued to escalate throughout 1999 and into the new millennium. These tensions eventually led to the NOAH exodus.

Motoko Baba was something of a divisive figure in Japan's pro wrestling industry. While Shohei

'Giant' Baba was beloved by fans and wrestlers alike, Motoko Baba garnered something of a bad reputation. According to Dave Meltzer, many wrestlers had 'a Motoko Baba story' or a reflection on times when they had found her challenging to deal with[61]. She was allegedly known as the 'Dragon Lady'.

It should be noted, however, that this reputation for ferocity was by design. In order to preserve Shohei 'Giant' Baba's image and legacy, the couple employed something of a 'good cop/bad cop' routine, with Motoko Baba becoming responsible for breaking bad news[62]. Putting it somewhat differently, Fumi Saito said in an interview that Motoko Baba's role was to be a 'firewall' for her husband. 'It wasn't entirely her fault,' he said, 'she always had to be a tough woman, being in a men's industry'.

Stan Hansen also believed gender may have been a factor in how Motoko Baba was perceived. In his book, *The Last Outlaw*, he observed she was a strong businesswoman, which may have itself upset some talent: 'Things in the company improved when Mrs Baba took over as office manager. Her organisational skills were part of the reason for All Japan making a turnaround, and over time, she became a powerful figure in the office.

'She was strong and she ran a very tight ship, directing the Japanese wrestlers and office staff more like a Japanese corporation. She also ran the marketing of products for the business. It really took a lot of stress and strain off Baba. Personally, she treated us all cordially and with respect. I heard some talk about her alienating the Japanese wrestlers, but I don't know what the conflict was about. It might have been due to the reality of Japan's male-dominated society'[63].

Hansen later recalled Motoko Baba's generosity towards All Japan's *gaijin* talent, which included flying in supplies such as turkey so the American wrestlers could celebrate Thanksgiving together while on tour. Displays such as this appear to have garnered a two-sided reputation for Baba, a powerful woman beloved by many of the foreign talent but viewed in less favourable terms by the native talent.

Problems between Mitsuharu Misawa and Motoko Baba were evident as early as 1996. As All Japan Pro Wrestling's popularity peaked, Baba was said to be sceptical of Misawa's contributions to ticket sales, attributing the promotion's success to the efforts of other talents, such as Kawada and Kobashi.

In 1997, the two needed to work together more often and in a formal way, as Shohei Baba made Misawa All Japan's new booker. As booker, Misawa was in an influential position, in charge of determining match finishes and long-term plans for the promotion's direction.

He was one of the key people determining which wrestlers held titles and who decided the company's future. If tensions between Motoko Baba and Mitsuharu Misawa bubbled under the surface during Misawa's run as booker, they became much more apparent in 1999 after tragedy struck.

During periods of awkwardness, Shohei 'Giant' Baba played peacekeeper between his wife and his protégé. However, he never informed Misawa he may well need to one day deal with Motoko without his mentor as an intermediary. When he was diagnosed with colon cancer, both Shohei and Motoko Baba agreed to keep the severity of his illness a closely guarded secret, with only a few people privy to the prognosis. This inner circle consisted of five members: Motoko, All Japan Pro Wrestling board member Sachiko, Baba's sister, referee Kyohei Wada, and Baba's personal secretary Ryu Nakata[64].

On 31 January 1999, Baba was rushed to Tokyo University Hospital, where he died due to complications from the cancer. He was sixty-one.

In Japan, it is not uncommon for private events such as illnesses, weddings, and even death, to be shielded from the public eye for a long time. Such was the case with Baba's passing, which Motoko took great care to shield from the attention of journalists and industry insiders.

The news caught most of All Japan's employees

and talent roster by surprise, including officials Joe Higuchi, Jumbo Tsuruta, and Misawa. Motoko Baba went to great pains to hide Baba's passing from public attention. This included telling one journalist who arrived on her doorstep that her husband was fine, while incense burned, part of the traditional rites after someone has passed away[65]. When the time came for a public announcement, All Japan called a press conference, where a visibly shaken Misawa confirming the news publicly.

Misawa became president of All Japan Pro Wrestling despite Motoko's wishes, as she had intended to make Mitsuo Momota president. She quickly found, however, that Misawa was foremost in most talents' minds as the best person for the job. He had the respect of his peers in the locker room due to his years of service in classic matches which had taken their toll on him.

'Vader [called] Misawa the star quarterback,' Saito said. 'He [was] a top wrestler, the locker room leader, and the leader of everybody. The kind of person that everybody would listen to'.

After a period of training for the role, Misawa took up the position. He raised eyebrows early on when he requested a desk to work at, something that Shohei Baba never had during his time running the company[66]. Misawa would indeed bring about changes to All Japan's front office.

In early 1999. All Japan Pro Wrestling board member Jumbo Tsuruta announced his retirement from wrestling, with a ceremony on 6 March. He left the company and Japan four days later.

An educated man with a master's degree in Coaching and a bachelor's degree in Political Science, Tsuruta's dream was to teach at a university. Making his way to the United States, he took up a role as a visiting researcher at the University of Portland in Oregon. Before Tsuruta left Japan, he let Misawa know that he was on his side and hoped that he might become All Japan president.

Upon his arrival in the United States, Tsuruta confirmed that there was a power struggle within All Japan's management, publicly declaring that Misawa should be named president and that Motoko Baba should be named as the company's owner.

While he was in the United States, Tsuruta's health deteriorated. Having been previously diagnosed with Hepatitis B, he developed liver cancer, as well as cirrhosis of the liver. In need of a transplant, he returned to Japan by the end of 1999. At the time, however, Japan's strict organ donation laws meant that he required a donor from his own family. On 11 April 2000, he left Japan once more for Australia. Tsuruta underwent an operation in Brisbane to try to remove the cancer and stayed there while he recuperated. He still needed a new liver and wanted to do so outside Japan or the US to ensure his privacy.

Eventually, Tsuruta found a donor in the Philippines, and he made his way to Manilla. On 13 May 2000, he underwent a transplant operation. During the operation, however, he developed complications, began to bleed uncontrollably, and passed away. He was forty-nine.

Most Japanese newspapers, radio stations, and television stations covered Tsuruta's death, noting his achievements as an amateur wrestler as well as his stardom in the professional ranks[67].

With Baba and Tsuruta, gone, Misawa and Baba clashed with no buffers between them.

Booking and money

According to the legendary wrestling announcer and former WWF head of talent, Jim Ross, disputes in professional wrestling come down to two things: cash and creative, an observation that Ross attributes to his mentor and former employer Vince McMahon[68].

A major source of the clash between Misawa and Baba was a difference of opinion regarding how the company could overcome its declining business. On one hand, Misawa wanted to modernise All Japan by booking new matchups with fresh stars, changing aspects of the company's presentation, and booking new buildings. On the other hand,

Motoko Baba wanted to retain All Japan Pro Wrestling's traditions, arguing (accurately) that the company's business had peaked during prior years.

Misawa focused on marketing the new and different, for example, when he booked two young stars, Jun Akiyama and Takao Omori, in the main event of a show at the Nippon Budokan. While the show sold out, and the exact match placement was left in the hands of a fan ballot, it nonetheless showed a willingness to build towards the company's future and to push newer names into the spotlight. Misawa's choice led to a disagreement between the two, as Baba believed that a Budokan show's main event should be either a tournament final or a Triple Crown match in, as had been the tradition. Nonetheless, Misawa prevailed, and booked five singles matches on the show[69].

Another example of Misawa shifting from tradition took place during the 1999 Champion Carnival, when he left the long-time tournament participant Stan Hansen on the sidelines in favour of younger talent and booked the *gaijin* heel Vader to win the tournament. Misawa made another big change to the Carnival a year later, when he changed the structure of the tournament from the traditional round-robin over two blocks, with the year 2000 version operating instead as a single elimination tournament, with Triple Crown Heavyweight Champion Kenta Kobashi winning.

Tension over the above subjects spilled into meetings and the backstage area. Summarising the dynamic between the Misawa and Baba, Hisame wrote, 'Both could be infuriatingly stubborn, both knew how to fight, and neither would give way'[70].

Grief may have also played a part in exasperating tensions. Misawa and Baba had both, in some sense, inherited All Japan Pro Wrestling, and with it, the struggle over whose ideas better represented Shohei Baba's vision for the company. Motoko wanted to ensure that Baba's vision for All Japan endured after his death. Misawa understood that Baba wanted him involved in company decision-making.

The medium of communication further aggravated tensions, especially when Motoko Baba was not physically present for many of the shows. As the *Wrestling Observer* reported, 'Misawa's complaint is that Motoko Baba never even comes to the shows anymore, but still won't give up her decision making power'[71].

Fumi Saito likened the struggle between Misawa and Baba to a Shakespearean struggle between grieving members of a royal family: 'When the king dies, who inherits the crown?'

In this clash, Motoko Baba had a good deal at stake when it came to her personal and professional reputation. 'She didn't want to be the widow that ran All Japan into the ground,' Saito said.

When it came to the 'cash' side of the business dispute, Misawa and Baba argued over a number of key financial subjects.

Misawa, for his part, wanted to modernise All Japan's contracts. In exchange for tying talent to binding deals, he wanted to provide the promotion's roster with bonuses, as well as healthcare and stock options[72].

The latter was not unheard of in wrestling, with the WWF (now WWE) providing its roster with stock during its Initial Public Offer in 1999. Wrestlers often did not entirely understand the implications of having stock, with former head of talent relations Jim Ross joking in his second autobiography that him explaining stocks to wrestlers was, 'like a turnip trying to teach a spoon the theory of relativity'[73].

Nonetheless, the extension of stock options was a policy that later proved popular as a source of additional income, and this was not confined to American companies. When it came to *puroresu*, New Japan Pro Wrestling also provided some of its contracted talent with stock options. Baba, however, remained firm in her belief that she should retain her eight-five percent ownership of the company's stock.

Another source of financial tension between the

two were a number of subsidiaries that Misawa discovered in his time as president. All Japan had a number of revenue streams, including ticket sales, videogames, merchandise, and outside appearance fees for the company's talent. Despite this, only the revenue generated by ticket sales made its way into All Japan itself, while the other revenue made its way directly into the subsidies. In a September 2000 interview, Misawa alleged that this money was lining the Baba family coffers[74].

In an interview conducted for this book, Fumi Saito said, while the subsidiaries were unknown to Misawa, there was nothing untoward or illegal about them. 'I am aware of the group companies All Japan Pro Wrestling, Giant Service, B&J, and King's Road,' Saito said. 'There are two sides to every story. All the merchandising money was to go into Giant Service, which was their baby company. All Japan was strictly a wrestling promotion. The boys never signed anything in writing on gimmick sales. [This was a] very old fashioned, outdated operation but that's how it had been since the beginning, I believe'.

Regardless of their legal status, All Japan Pro Wrestling's financial structures were a point of contention, and Misawa believed that his position within the company was becoming untenable. Before this tension could be resolved, however, Misawa had other tasks to tend to.

Paying tribute to Giant Baba

As All Japan Pro Wrestling's president, Misawa needed to help prepare the company's tribute to his predecessor and fallen mentor, Shohei 'Giant' Baba.

Before the 1999 Champion Carnival Final, All Japan hosted a fan event on 17 April at the Nippon Budokan, where 28,000 people left flowers in the ring.

On 2 May 1999, All Japan Pro Wrestling ran a posthumous 'retirement' show for Giant Baba in the Tokyo Dome. The promotion went to great pains to emphasise that this was not a memorial show, and that such a show was slated for a later date[75]. Instead, the show was presented as though Baba was going to once again headline in the retirement match that death had denied him. Amongst the nostalgia, Misawa's booking continued to build the next generation of All Japan Pro Wrestling stars. One of these was a young Naomichi Marufuji, who teamed with Tsuyoshi Kikuchi to beat Gran Naniwa and Makoto Hashi.

During the match, Marufuji was presented as Giant Baba's last student, opening his trainer's retirement show. As with so many other things in professional wrestling, this was not entirely true. While Marufuji trained in the All Japan dojo, a training facility in Baba's purview, the recent high school graduate received his wrestling education from Misawa. Baba's last direct student was Jun Akiyama. As it would turn out, only part of Marufuji's great potential was ever realised in Baba's company.

In a 'match' deemed to be Giant Baba's retirement bout in absentia, the Destroyer 'teamed' with Baba in what was dubbed as a tag team match against Gene Kiniski and Bruno Sammartino. The Destroyer, Kiniski, and Sammartino lined up in the ring while footage played of all three's in-ring encounters with Baba. All three paid tribute to their fallen comrade and former boss. Baba's size twenty-three boots were placed in the ring while a ten-bell salute played, a traditional ritual of mourning in the professional wrestling industry[76].

In a violent and suitably dramatic main event, Misawa defeated Vader to capture the Triple Crown. In the post-match promo, the new champion told the crowd, 'Tonight, Baba retired. He may be gone, but to me, he'll always be the boss'. While fans were not aware of the subtext, these words were a foreshadowing of Misawa's upcoming exit from the promotion that Baba had founded back in 1972 during his own defection from the JWA[77].

The significance behind this statement became apparent a little over a year later. With Misawa and Baba continuing to fight over the company's direction, things were at an impasse. The company's owner sought to resolve this. On 28 May 2000, she introduced a motion to the company's board to remove Misawa as president. The majority voted with her. Misawa was gone.

Conclusion to Chapter Three

With All Japan Pro Wrestling's business down from its prior heights, Mitsuharu Misawa and Motoko Baba clashed over the company's future direction, with prior disagreements giving way to open enmity between the pair. With the need for a circuit breaker, Motoko led the company's board in removing Misawa. Misawa responded to this removal in a way that few could have expected, including Baba. Misawa's press conference contained a bombshell announcement and ended with All Japan Pro Wrestling facing closure.

CHAPTER FOUR: THE SPLIT

From early 2000, the *Wrestling Observer* and other outlets reported that Mitsuharu Misawa planned to leave All Japan Pro Wrestling and form his own company (Meltzer, 2000a). Ever since Misawa took up the role of All Japan booker in 1997, there had been conflict between he and Motoko Baba, with this only intensifying when Misawa took up the role of the company's president in 1999.

In February 2000, the rumour made print in *Weekly Fight Magazine*, with the suggestion that Misawa could leave All Japan as early as May to form his own promotion. Misawa pointedly refused to comment on the matter and tensions persisted all the way up to 28 May 2000, the day the board dismissed him from his corporate role.

Very soon after the board voted to remove him, Misawa began speaking to All Japan talent backstage, telling them that he intended to leave the promotion and form his own company. He also personally approached trainees in All Japan Pro Wrestling's dojo. Misawa asked them to trust him and join him on this journey[78].

In keeping with the tradition of not wanting to lose face, all of these events were kept quiet as All Japan's day-to-day business continued. All parties had agreed to keep Misawa's removal a closely guarded secret until after the current tour had finished. In an attempt to preserve Giant Baba's legacy, along with that of the recently deceased Jumbo Tsuruta, Misawa asked Motoko Baba to give her blessing to begin a new company. For her part, Baba refused[79].

According to Fumi Saito, Misawa did not anticipate the level of support that he received from his peers. Initially, he expected enough support to create a small company that grew from the grassroots with four or five other talents. 'Initially, he was just going to take a couple of guys. Not to destroy All Japan,' Saito said[80].

Instead, Misawa found that an overwhelming majority of the company's wrestlers and staff supported him. Provided they saw out their obligations to All Japan and honoured existing match bookings until late-July 2000, many wrestlers were able to leave without legal obstacles or ramifications.

Misawa approached trainees and asked them to join the group that was leaving. As a result, a number of future stars left All Japan, some of them having never wrestled in front of an audience. Takashi Sugiura, Kenta Kobayashi (later known as KENTA), Yoshinobu Kanemaru, Naomichi Marufuji, Takeshi Rikio, and others representing the next generation of pro wrestling in Japan joined their trainers in walking out.

As well as current wrestlers and trainees, office staff and senior officials looked to leave All Japan. Twelve staff members left with the intent of joining Misawa's new start-up. Among them were long time All Japan referee and official Joe Higuchi, Mitsuo Momota, and Yoshiro Momota.

Joe Higuchi was a significant loss for All Japan. As well as refereeing historic bouts, he played a significant role, especially for the company's foreign talent. In addition to assisting with translation during press conferences, Higuchi was an essential link between the office and the *gaijin* locker room. He took talents' complaints and concerns to the Babas, helped the wrestlers find their way around Japan, and answered any questions they had. Whenever a *gaijin* talent found themselves in trouble, Higuchi was quickly on the scene to iron out the problem.

As Stan Hansen put it: 'Joe-san stepped in so many times to help *gaijins* who had gotten themselves into trouble. I phrase it that way because most of the time, the *gaijins* were at fault. There were times when trouble just seemed to find us, but most of the time, it was our fault. I can't think of one *gaijin* who didn't get some kind of help from Joe-san in situations like the ones described above, including me'[81].

Mitsuo Momota, and Yoshiro Momota were the sons of legendary Japanese pro wrestler, Rikidōzan. Both of them played a significant role in the formation of All Japan, leaving the JWA alongside Giant Baba. Though they took decades of experience in the wrestling industry with them, in Yoshiro Momota's case, this was a short-term endeavour. After suffering from liver failure, he passed away on 22 September 2000 at the age of fifty-four.

On 16 June 2000, the recently deposed Mitsuharu Misawa called a press conference. He was surrounded by the majority of All Japan's native roster. Over 100 media agencies attended the conference, held at Differ Ariake. The gathered journalists were keen to hear what Misawa had to say. All eyes were on the former All Japan president.

An emotional Misawa's read out a statement to the gathered journalists. This initial comment was brief but decisive:

As you all already know, I, Mitsuharu Misawa, have resigned as an officer of All Japan Pro Wrestling. I have also given my notice that I will not be re-signing my contract as a wrestler. In other words, I am leaving All Japan.

For about one year, I have tried my best as president to continue the legend of AJPW, however, I feel there is a disconnect between AJPW and the type of wrestling that I want to do in the future. In order to stick to my wrestling ideals, and not to destroy the AJPW that Baba-san created, I have decided to leave.

Regarding my next step, I will be creating a new promotion with the roster that has joined me here today. To the media, staff, and fans, I, along with the rest of the roster, apologise for the trouble and worry we may have created. We are planning to do our best from the start. We appreciate your continued support, thank you[82].

Motoko Baba held a press conference of her own on 16 June. The All Japan owner announced a number of *gaijin* talent were joining Fuchi and Kawada on the promotion's July tour, which was going on as scheduled.

She went on the defensive with a statement that accused Misawa's group of wrestlers of disloyalty. Baba claimed that Misawa hadn't worked hard as company president over the past year and that he had been planning to leave for some time. She also mentioned a one million dollar loan Misawa had taken out, and then quickly repaid to the company, arguing that the quick repayment was proof he had intended to leave.

Despite entering into this war of words with Misawa, Baba invited the wrestlers who were leaving to join the tour and work with the company one last time before their departure. Baba indicated that she was waiting to hear back from Misawa before announcing the tour's line-up.

As *The Wrestling Observer* put it, 'This was a political move, just as Misawa had made, to babyface the promotion in the fans' eyes that even though the wrestlers left, she was trying to do everything to book strong cards for the July tour'[83].

In a radio interview not long afterwards, Baba's tone was that of a disappointed mother. Motoko also said that when Giant Baba was alive the pair got along, but that after he died, Misawa changed. She added that she could not believe that Misawa, 'whose father (Baba) loved him would do something like this'[84].

On 17 June, Misawa announced that his new promotion now had a name. It was to be known as Pro Wrestling NOAH. He followed this up with another press conference eleven days later, where he announced that the new company's first two shows were planned to run back-to-back on 5 and 6 August in Differ Ariake, the promotion's new home.

Appropriately enough, the shows were promoted under the name 'Departure'. In a visual nod to the original JWA split that formed All Japan, all of the wrestlers defecting to NOAH took a photo on a staircase, this time on the steps outside Differ Ariake. The message here was clear: Misawa was following in Baba's footsteps in his own way, by leading his own promotional exodus.

For those departing the company, the name symbolised the Genesis flood narrative, and the journey from danger to the safety of new land.

On 19 June, All Japan Pro Wrestling held another press conference. Kawada and Fuchi fronted reporters and confirmed that they were staying with Baba.

In a symbolic blow to the company, all of All Japan Pro Wrestling's championships were vacated. Kenta Kobashi relinquished the Triple Crown, The Holy Demon Army let go of the World Tag Team Championships, Tamon Honda and Masao Inoue gave up the All Asia Tag Team Championships, and Yoshinari Ogawa vacated the World Junior Heavyweight title. All Japan Pro Wrestling needed to hold off on finding replacements until they stabilised their roster.

It was not only wrestlers who left to join Misawa's new promotion. After a mass resignation from the front office, All Japan's remaining employees included Motoko Baba, Kyohei Wada, the company's PR agent, and their ring announcer.

Showcasing the company during this rebuilding

process was made all the more difficult by another detail in the split. Misawa did not just walk out with the majority of All Japan's roster and office. In a further echo of Giant Baba's JWA exodus, Misawa met with representatives from Nippon TV (NTV) and secured All Japan's television timeslot for NOAH. Operating from midnight on Friday under the name 'Collesseo', the program featured weekly tapings from Misawa's new promotion, along with roundup coverage of All Japan[85]. While hardly prime time viewing, television was a major avenue of visibility and income for a new brand that was quickly gathering momentum.

For All Japan, the loss of their television deal was another brutal blow and the end of an era. NTV had covered the promotion since its 1972 launch, making it one of the longest-running TV partnerships in pro wrestling history. The loss of NTV had implications beyond historical significance. In Japan, the channels that broadcast wrestling shows oftentimes film the shows, thereby owning the rights to the footage in the long term, and frequently invest in the company itself[86]. As a result, NTV still owned the rights to All Japan's shows up to 2000 despite the split, and their fifteen percent stake in the promotion ensured that any efforts to find a new provider were complicated.

Several analysts argued at the time that the loss

of All Japan's NTV deal signalled the end of the company. There was certainly historical precedent for this: both the JWA and Isao Yoshiwara's International Wrestling Enterprise (IWE) went under after losing their television deals.

The last tour

While Toshiaki Kawada and Masanobu Fuchi were the only native members of All Japan Pro Wrestling's permanent roster who opted to stay with the company, the majority of *gaijin* talent remained, including Maunakea Mossman, Mike Barton, 'Dr Death' Steve Williams, Johnny Smith, Jim Steele, Mike Rotunda, and George Hines. Vader, Scorpio, and Richard Slinger all eventually joined Misawa's group of departing wrestlers. As Dave Meltzer pointed out at the time, 'Since most of the foreigners were not involved in the Misawa/Motoko Baba dispute and their business dealings were through the office, their loyalties lay with Shohei Baba and sided with Motoko'[87].

Stan Hansen opted to remain loyal to Baba but was limited to wrestling a few times a year and eyeing retirement. Rather than choosing either side, Johnny Ace retired from the ring and left Japan for a backstage role with WCW. Later, when WCW was purchased by the WWF, Ace went on to be one of the agents hired by McMahon and his Japanese ties saw a number of outgoing WWF wrestlers booked in All Japan. Hiroshi Hase, by then a member of the House of Representatives in the National Diet, was another part-time worker with a decision to make about where he would take future bookings.

Ever the consummate politician, Hase allegedly gave undertakings to wrestle for both All Japan and Pro Wrestling NOAH in due course. He stuck with Baba for the immediate future as his political career allowed and made his NOAH debut at a later date[88].

A final tour featured a mix of those who were departing for NOAH and those remaining with All Japan. On 20 July 2000, Yoshinobu Kanemaru, Takeshi Morishima, Naomichi Marufuji, Kentaro Shiga, Takeshi Rikio, Mitsuo Momota, Rusher Kimura, Haruka Eigen, Tsuyoshi Kikuchi, Kenta Kobayashi, Takao Omori, Yoshihiro Takayama, Jun Izumida, Masao Inoue, Yoshinari Ogawa, Akira Taue, Jun Akiyama, and Mitsuharu Misawa competed in their last matches for All Japan Pro Wrestling. The show took place at the Hakata Star Lane in Fukuoka, an old, converted bowling alley now used for professional wrestling that held some 2,000 fans.

The final tour featured a 'wall' between All Japan wrestlers and the departing NOAH talent. They did not meet in the ring or outside of it, with All Japan stars wrestling All Japan stars, and NOAH departees doing the same thing[89].

During the final show to feature the departing stars, All Japan *gaijin* 'Dr Death' Steve Williams walked out and shook hands with Misawa, asking for one final singles match. As soon as the final match with NOAH-bound talent had taken place, however, Misawa joined all of his talent on the bus and departed for Differ, leaving behind the tensions between him and Baba before the final two matches even hit the ring.

With an unprecedented number of wrestlers leaving with Misawa, the wrestling industry was convinced that All Japan Pro Wrestling was not going to last much longer, a belief that is evident in commentary and reporting from the time. In the wake of Misawa securing his former promotion's time slot, *Slam Wrestling*'s John F. Molinaro wrote that: 'According to Japanese wrestling observers and officials within the company itself, the cancellation of the TV program, the backbone of All Japan pro wrestling, spells the end for the promotion. It is expected that the July 23 show booked at Tokyo's Nippon Budokan Hall will be the last ever All Japan show as company officials are telling All Japan owner Motoko Baba to throw in the towel'[90].

Despite this considerable pressure from within her company, Motoko Baba was not one for giving up easily. Preserving All Japan Pro Wrestling was an imperative for her and a way to honour the legacy of her late husband. To ensure the company's survival, Baba needed an ambitious plan that provide wrestling fans with something to talk about, to reframe what had taken place and change the narrative that wrestling fans had: namely that All Japan was a promotion in decline.

Conclusion to Chapter Four

After years of tension between Mitsuharu Misawa and Motoko Baba, All Japan Pro Wrestling finally split into two smaller companies. With their roster and office decimated, rumours swirled that the company was going to close. With all eyes on Misawa's new venture, Pro Wrestling NOAH, All Japan Pro Wrestling needed to do something big in order to change the prevailing narrative and survive. For her next move, Motoko Baba reached out to an unexpected source for help. Later, she reached out to a traditional rival for help.

CHAPTER FIVE: SURVIVAL

With all but two of All Japan Pro Wrestling's native stars having left for Pro Wrestling NOAH, along with a large portion of its office staff and TV deal, a number of media outlets were openly questioning whether or not the company would survive[91] [92]. The company started by Shohei 'Giant' Baba in 1972 had endured defections before, including in 1990, when Genichiro Tenryu left, taking a number of key talents to form Super World of Sports (SWS).

The SWS defection allowed for All Japan to re-organise around the efforts of young stars Misawa, Kobashi, Kawada, and Taue. The formation of Pro Wrestling NOAH was more brutal, however, as it took wrestlers from the company's past (the Momoto brothers), its present (three of the Four Pillars, including Triple Crown Champion Kenta Kobashi) and its future (trainees such as Naomichi Marufuji, Takeshi Rikio, Takashi Sugiura, and Kenta Kobayashi).

Toshiaki Kawada and Masanobu Fuchi were the two central stars who decided to stay with All Japan. According to Kawada, Misawa didn't give him any choice, keeping the plans for NOAH's launch from him until the press conference. Kawada suggested, however, that he appreciated Misawa's decision. 'We had been together through good and bad since high school,' Kawada said. 'He was one year my senior, so he always had that mindset of being the boss. [Separating] was something I knew he hated to do, but that I'd always wanted'[93].

Misawa and Kawada had a long professional rivalry over who was the number one star in the promotion. At times, tensions bubbled over, and the two engaged in several backstage fights. Separating gave Kawada the challenge, as well as the opportunity, to step out of Misawa's shadow.

Fumi Saito believes that if Misawa had personally asked Kawada to join NOAH, he likely would have left with the other departing talent. 'Kawada did not want to hear about this new company from someone else. If he heard from Misawa, he would have gone,' Saito said. While wrestling folklore has long suggested that Misawa and Kawada had a falling out around the time of the split over an unspecified issue, Saito believes that this was not the case. 'They were brothers,' he said.

Unlike their Japanese counterparts, the majority of

All Japan's foreign talents opted to remain with Motoko Baba's promotion. While Vader, Scorpio, and Richard Slinger all eventually made their way to Misawa's new promotion, the majority of the *gaijin* locker room were mostly distanced from the conflict driving the split and content to remain with the company that gave them a working environment that was relatively free from the politics and stress that sometimes plagued the American wrestling product.

Stan Hansen was one of the *gaijin* who opted to stay with All Japan. As he later wrote, the former Triple Crown Champion was loyal to Motoko Baba: 'Soon after Baba passed away and Mrs Baba took over, Leon [Vader] and others moved towards Mitsuharu Misawa's power play and away from Mrs Baba. I chose to stick with Mrs Baba. It was not a hard choice. Mrs Baba was Baba-san's wife, and Baba-san was my friend, first and foremost. I don't knock anyone for doing what they think is best for their career, but [the] old saying "where money lies, honour dies" seemed to ring true during that time'[94].

While Hansen was near retirement, his decision to stay, and his comments about the split are illustrative of the divide that existed between the Japanese talent and most of their *gaijin* counterparts when it came to Baba. While many of the native wrestlers sided with Misawa, the *gaijin* talent did not have the same problems with her.

One of the other foreign talents who stayed with All Japan, former Junior Heavyweight Champion Maunakea Mossman, said that a conversation with Motoko Baba clarified his thoughts. 'Tours were still going on when they were talking about it,' he recalled. 'It didn't happen right away.'

For Mossman, who had joined the All Japan dojo at the age of eighteen, shortly after graduating high school, the decision to stay with the company was one that came down to loyalty. 'Talking to Mrs Baba...I remember thinking about it and going, "I wouldn't be here if not for Mr Baba, you know, everything he taught me." He was a great guy,' he said.

'I remember that first show right afterwards [following the split] and just how odd and different it was'[95].

Mossman saw an opportunity to reinvent himself and up his stock. Shaving his head and adopting new tights, he changed his in-ring name to Taiyō Kea. His loyalty to the company was rewarded with a steady upward climb that eventually culminated in him winning the Triple Crown Heavyweight Championship, becoming the first man to ever hold both the junior heavyweight and heavyweight championships.

All Japan's most famous referee, Kyohei Wada, was one of the few key staff members who elected to stay in the company, apparently refusing to even hear any mention of the possible exodus before it took place.

Wada was one of Motoko Baba's supporters, who understood that her reputation was the result of the perceived need to take on the role of stern mother in contrast to Giant Baba's image as the beloved father. 'She was a mother to me,' he wrote. 'Her and Giant Baba were flip sides of the same coin. You have a face and a heel in wrestling, and theirs was the same relationship. She knew nobody could think ill of Baba and made him stronger by being tough'[96].

All Japan also turned to unsigned talent from the independent scene to fill out their cards. In Japanese wrestling, these freelancers can find themselves in demand from multiple promotions. One key freelancer during this period was Jinsei Shinzaki, a wrestler from Michinoku Pro Wrestling who had previously wrestled in America as Hakushi. Another freelancer familiar to international audiences was Rob Van Dam, who joined a few tours between the end of ECW and the beginning of his WWF run.

There were a few wrestlers whose defection to Pro Wrestling NOAH did not last. Masahito Kakihara initially joined Misawa's new promotion. He wrestled one match for NOAH on 5 August before he resigned, later re-joining All Japan in October as a freelancer.

In addition to those loyal talents who stayed, and the freelancers that All Japan could rely on to fill out its cards, the promotion needed a circuit breaker. With the prevalent narrative that the company was dying, Motoko Baba needed talent who could generate some much-needed hype and challenge negative perceptions. Ironically enough, the owner of All Japan Pro Wrestling found herself reaching out to someone who had previously deserted the promotion, asking if he was willing to re-join his old home.

Using the golden hour

One key theory in crisis communication is the notion of the 'golden hour', a short period of time that an organisation has when it can still respond to a situation and take control of the surrounding narrative. As Helio Fred Garcia writes, 'The Golden Hour doesn't refer to a particular number of minutes but rather the observation that incremental delays in controlling the communication agenda lead to greater-than-incremental harm'[97]. In order to do this, and spark interest in All Japan Pro Wrestling's product, Motoko Baba needed to respond swiftly to the crisis at hand and reach out to someone who could help. Her solution was something unexpected that, if successful, promised to generate positive headlines and frame All Japan as a promotion still worthy of fans' attention. Ironically enough, she found herself reaching out to someone who had previously deserted All Japan, to see if he might re-join them.

Using a common contact, Baba called Genichiro Tenryu. Being the second ever Triple Crown Heavyweight Champion and someone who had a proven track record as a draw and performer, Tenryu was an important part of the company's history. Getting him to be a central part of the post-split era of All Japan created fresh matchups.

Thankfully for Motoko Baba, Tenryu agreed to return. According to Fumi Saito, the fact that Baba personally called him was a deciding factor. 'She was the one who actually picked up the phone,' Saito said. 'She never trusted the middle person.' Another large reason for Tenryu's decision was that he was keen to test himself in a match with Kawada, who was his former protégé and the last remaining native wrestler who was a main event level attraction.

At the time, Tenryu was still technically the head of a declining promotion known as Wrestling Association R (formerly known as Wrestling And Romance, WAR). While the company had ceased running regular shows and had released talent from their contracts, there were nonetheless still wrestlers that Tenryu knew that he could rely upon. Officially closing WAR, he also brought several talents with him, including Nobukazu Harai and Nobutaka Araya. Later he teamed up with old rival Yoji Anjo, who had joined All Japan as a freelancer.

On 2 July 2000, Motoko Baba surprised the audience at a Korakuen Hall show by walking to the ring with Toshiaki Kawada, Masanobu Fuchi, and Maunaukea Mossman in tow. An emotional Baba thanked fans for their ongoing support of All Japan to polite applause. She then surprised the audience with an announcement that Genichiro Tenryu was returning to All Japan, a statement that elicited a gasp from the audience. When Tenryu's music played, the audience chanted loudly.

The second Triple Crown champion re-entered his old promotion and shook hands with those gathered in the ring. He then left without directly addressing the audience, his actions having said as much as needed to be said.

Tenryu's first match back with his former company took place on 23 July. More than a decade since his last All Japan match, Tenryu teamed with Toshiaki Kawada to defeat Mossman (shortly before he changed his name to Taiyō Kea) and Stan Hansen in the main event of a show at the Nippon Budokan.

As the promotion's biggest two names, a series of matches between Tenryu and Kawada was inevitable. As previously noted, the departure of the majority of the roster to NOAH meant that All Japan needed to book some tournaments to crown new champions for all of their belts. Over the course of a month, the promotion waged a tournament to crown a new Triple Crown Heavyweight Champion, to shore up its main events and give the company a leader who set the in-ring standard.

Kawada and Tenryu were joined by Stan Hansen, Mike Barton, Shiro Koshinaka, 'Dr Death' Steve Williams, Johnny Smith, and Jinsei Shinzaki in an eight-man tournament. The promotion also brought in Gene Kininski to present the belts to the eventual winner. This was a nod to history, as Kininski was a former NWA International Champion who had wrestled Giant Baba for sixty-five minutes in one of the All Japan founder's greatest matches[98].

On 28 October 2000, the tournament final finally took place at the Budokan. As Dave Meltzer writes, Genichiro Tenryu proved instrumental to the survival of his new promotional home, with the Kawada match in the Budokan proving a financial and critical success: 'It was a show when a few months back it was debatable if the company would even last long enough to have one after most of its top stars in the company left with Mitsuharu Misawa to form Pro Wrestling NOAH.'

Instead, due to the acquisition of Tenryu, the promotion created some fresh, short-term marquee matchups and marked the company's third consecutive Budokan Hall sell-out since the defections. In what the *Wrestling Observer* suggested was a four star match, Tenryu pinned Kawada in 26:28 after a hard lariat, his trademark punch to the face that Kawada sold as a near knockout, and a Northern lights bomb. Tenryu was bleeding from the nose by the closing minutes and had near falls after several *enzuigiris*. After the match, Gene Kiniski presented Tenryu with the three belts, the old NWA International heavyweight, the old PWF heavyweight and the old NWA United National heavyweight'[99].

Tenryu, and All Japan Pro Wrestling, were here to stay. The company finally had a new Triple Crown Champion to replace Kobashi.

The World Tag Team Championship was settled a few months later, when the newly renamed Taiyō Kea and Johnny Smith defeated Fuchi and Kawada on 14 January 2001. The following June, Masahito Kakihara and Mitsuya Nagai lifted the secondary All-Asian Tag Team Championship.

The World Junior Heavyweight Championship took longer to fill, however, and remained vacant until April 2002. The rebuilding of these championships was a steady process that took place as All Japan established its roster. As symbols of competition, they played an important part in demonstrating that the promotion was on its way back from the brink.

An unheard-of alliance

Motoko Baba also reached out to another past rival to keep All Japan afloat. This time, it was a rival promotion that she called upon. New Japan Pro Wrestling had worked with Giant Baba sporadically, generally through brief talent exchanges, or in the context of rare inter-promotional shows such as the 1990 Wrestling Summit at the Tokyo Dome (which also featured the WWF and was the result of inter-promotional politics)[100]. Otherwise, relations between Japan's biggest wrestling promotions swung between friendly competition to outright hostility. In 2000, however, New Japan and All Japan agreed to cooperate as part of a formal working relationship, an alliance unheard of during Giant Baba's day.

On 11 August 2000, Fuchi surprised a New Japan Pro Wrestling audience by walking out to the ring and pledging to 'break the walls down that have long existed between us'[101]. New Japan's Ricki Choshu responded by walking down to the ring and shaking Fuchi's hand, signifying the beginning of a working relationship. In typical professional wrestling fashion, this was not a peaceful exchange of pleasantries, with the heel Team 2000 walking down to the ring to insult Fuchi and the roster that he represented.

The animosity that previously existed between the two promotions was now being turned into an on-air storyline. The two companies started to work together from that point. The first inter-promotional match between them in over a decade drew 16,300 people to the Budokan on 2 September, for a match pitting Masahiro Chono against Masa Fuchi.

This was a remarkable short-term turnaround for an All Japan show, with Dave Meltzer writing, 'The All Japan promotion, which was practically given its last rites when nearly all its talent quit, has now been saved and has great short-term business prospects with the opening of the feud with New Japan'[102].

The promotions' attention turned next towards planning and promoting New Japan's 9 October Tokyo Dome show, *Do Judge*. The show's main event was a heated clash between the IWGP Heavyweight Champion Kensuke Sasaki and All Japan's ace, Toshiaki Kawada.

In terms of the important live gate figures, *Do Judge* was a big success that demonstrated what the rivalry between the two promotions could achieve with the right build.

Fans were intrigued to see the clash between Sasaki and Kawada, as All Japan and New Japan had never cooperated to this extent before. As Dave Meltzer wrote, 'The show ended up being the thirteenth largest verifiable crowd in the history of pro wrestling, drawing a sell-out 64,000 fans paying an estimated $5.8 million'[103].

As part of the show was broadcast on TV Asahi, the station that owns the rights to New Japan's footage, it was not featured on pay per view (PPV). Meltzer viewed this decision as a costly mistake, as the event, 'likely would have been the biggest PPV event ever in Japan'[104]. It was not only All Japan that benefited from the working relationship, with New Japan enjoying the fruits of cooperation.

The Sasaki/Kawada match itself was a violent spectacle with a mystique enhanced by the two companies' long rivalry. From brutal strikes to submissions and unpredictable exchanges, the match had a lot for long-term fans of both strong style and King's Road matches. The sole point during which fans appeared to lose interest was when Kawada locked in the Stretch Plum, which he had not really used in years.

After Kawada pinned Sasaki to end the non-title match, the IWGP Heavyweight Champion took the title belt and left it in the ring, vacating it after he lost to an outsider.

The match won *Tokyo Sports*' and *Nikkan Sports*'

awards for Match of the Year and was recognised by New Japan Pro Wrestling as the company's official pick for the year's best singles bout.

All Japan came out two to one in inter-promotional match results, with 'Dr Death' Steve Williams defeating Scott Norton, while New Japan's Team 2000 defeated Masanobu Fuchi and Shiro Koshinaka.

With its acclaimed main event, record live gate, and overall buzz, *Do Judge* symbolised the potential of a relationship between the two promotions. It also showed, however, that the relationship was not free from politics and the associated problems and ego that so often end working relationships in the wrestling industry. The original intention behind the show's ending was to set up an eventual champion versus champion match.

As well as providing fans with an interesting, previously unheard of feud, the working relationship between All Japan and New Japan helped Motoko Baba fill out some early post-split cards. One of the major events that made heavy use of the working relationship was the Giant Baba Memorial show that All Japan promoted on 28 January 2001.

The memorial show, entitled *Oudou Shin Seiki* (King's Road New Century) 2001, took place two years after Giant Baba passed away. This marked a significant occasion, as in Japanese culture, the two-year point is a key time in grieving someone who has died.

Baba's memorial show featured New Japan stars Steve Williams, Kensuke Sasaki, and Jushin Thunder Liger, among others. However, political machinations regarding the card's matches showed that cooperation had its limits and that there were pitfalls to working with other promotions. The major source of disagreement surrounded plans for the show's last match.

The original plan was for Toshiaki Kawada to win the IWGP Heavyweight Championship and face Genichiro Tenryu for both New Japan's belt and the Triple Crown. After New Japan management cooled on the idea of having an outsider win their main prize, they booked Sasaki to defeat Kawada in a rematch on 4 January. The main event of *Oudou Shin Seiki* was changed to a tag team match pitting Kawada and Kesuke Sasaki against Tenryu and Hiroshi Hase.

The show's 'main event' slot was reserved, not for a match, but for a retirement ceremony. At fifty-one years of age, Stan Hansen had provided decades of service to the wrestling industry, especially to All Japan. During a Triple Crown tournament semi-final with Tenryu, Hansen was legitimately knocked unconscious. Unable to remember how the match ended, he took the event as 'a sign from God that I had to stop.' As soon as he showered and changed clothes, Hansen went directly to Baba and told her that he was going to retire[105].

In a short and simple retirement ceremony at the Tokyo Dome, Hansen thanked Baba, his promotion, and the fans that had supported him throughout his long career. In his book, Hansen remembered the retirement ceremony as an emotional event: 'Going to and from the ring with thousands of people chanting my name, "Hansen! Hansen! Hansen!" was something I can't even describe. I've heard that over the years, but I must say, that time, it really hit an emotional chord with me...I can never give back what they have given to me, not only that night, but through all the years I wrestled in Japan'[106].

Hansen had held on for a little while after the split and had provided Baba's promotion with his last few matches. As Dave Meltzer wrote, 'If you factor in longevity and everything else, Hansen would probably have to rank as the biggest foreign star ever to work in Japan, which is why his retirement is a big deal, especially coming on the heels of All Japan losing both Baba and Tsuruta, and basically most of its company, over the past two years'[107].

From 26 September 1975 to the retirement ceremony on 28 January 2001, Hansen completed 131 tours of Japan. Having amassed this amazing feat, he did not ride off into the sunset, opting to serve in a non-wrestling role as the president of the Pacific Wrestling Federation. This figurehead position involved reading the ceremony scroll before championship matches. Hansen recalled, 'I was just a figurehead with no power, but it was an easy job and I enjoyed keeping my hand in the business...I never looked at the position as anything but a gift, and I was happy to make the "easy money"'[108].

In the longer term, the All Japan/New Japan relationship provided All Japan with key talents that helped the company as Hansen stepped away from the ring. These men were Keiji Mutoh and Satoshi Kojima: future Triple Crown Heavyweight Champions and stars that All Japan could turn to in the next stage of the rebuilding process.

Enter Mutoh

Keiji Mutoh was a man in dire need of a change of scenery. Returning to New Japan Pro Wrestling after finding himself dismayed by WCW's mismanagement[109], he found himself once more questioning his career trajectory. Returning to New Japan on 31 December 2000, Mutoh appeared with a new look, complete with a shaved head and goatee. Taking full advantage of the working relationship, Mutoh formed a faction in early 2001 with members from both promotions. Bad Ass Translate Trading (BATT) was oddly named, but was far from a joke, including members such as Mutoh, Taiyō Kea, Don Frye, Shinjiro Otani, Hiroshi Hase, and

Jinsei Shinzaki.

On 8 June 2001, a little over a year after the split, Mutoh had a match that had people talking about All Japan. This match, for Tenryu's Triple Crown Heavyweight Championship, took a layered, slow burn approach, building in action and crowd support along the way.

Mutoh was physically limited. Years of hitting his signature moonsault from the top rope had taken their toll on his knees, and after a hip replacement nearly twenty years later , he reflected that he had been in pain. As Fumi Saito said, the match's layout worked to hide these physical limitations.

'When [Mutoh] couldn't do a big dropkick, he created [the basement dropkick],'he said. 'The next week everyone was doing it. Muto was always a trendsetter...He came up with things that no one else could,' Saito said.

As well as selling out the Nippon Budokan, Genichiro Tenryu vs Keiji, Mutoh earned the *Wrestling Observer* award for Match of the Year 2001. Less than a year after All Japan's future was in doubt, the promotion was producing a match deemed a must-see by respected wrestling publications.

When Mutoh won the match after his signature moonsault, it signalled a new phase in the New Japan/All Japan relationship, as a talent from the former company had won the other promotion's world title. This level of cooperation between the two promotions was unprecedented but did not last.

One event that complicated the relationship was an offer New Japan made to Baba to buy All Japan. According to Fumi Saito, 'It is a well-known fact within the Japanese wrestling community that New Japan Pro Wrestling wanted to buy All Japan Pro Wrestling in 2001. That is why New Japan Pro Wrestling sent stars like Masa Chono to All Japan Pro Wrestling's Nippon Budokan show. Fans always love cross promotion match ups.

'It was Katsuji Nagashima, then NJPW executive, and his guys' plan. It fell apart quickly because Motoko Baba simply did not trust Nagashima'.

Whether it entered Motoko Baba's mind or not, a similar situation took place on American soil that same year, when the World Wrestling Federation (WWF) bought their main competitor, World Championship Wrestling (WCW).

Vince McMahon now dominated North America, and, with it, the global broadcast wrestling product that many fans around the world were familiar with. Within less than a year, plans to relaunch WCW were abandoned, which Saito believes would also have been the case if New Japan bought the promotion they had competed against so ferociously since 1972.

'If Nagashima's plan had worked, they were going to have two brands, NJPW and AJPW, under one umbrella. But this type of plan would never work in wrestling. The rest of NJPW would want to demolish AJPW for good because that's what they fought to achieve for decades. They would never co-exist as equals. By then, AJPW's 1990s super stars were all gone. Of course, NJPW would destroy them with a good storyline. Probably, Motoko could see through that as well'.

While New Japan never publicly announced their intention to purchase their old rival, the story that they sought to was featured in Japanese professional wrestling publications.

Shortly after All Japan rebuffed New Japan's offer to buy their competition, Nagashima, along with Ricki Choshu, Masa Saito, Kensuke Sasaki, Kenzo Suzuki and others ended up leaving New Japan to form another ill-fated company, World Japan Pro Wrestling.

In January 2002, the inter-promotional cooperation between New Japan and All Japan came to an end. It was not the last time that the two companies worked together, however. New Japan Pro Wrestling's management changed a number of times, and the two companies eventually teamed up again to co-promote the first Wrestle Kingdom in the Tokyo Dome on 4 January 2007.

The 2002 end to the working relationship wound things up for the time being, as Baba did not see the angle as being one that should last longer. Keiji Mutoh was not done with All Japan, however. Shocking the wrestling world, he officially defected, bringing Satoshi Kojima and Kendo Kashin with him.

According to Saito, Mutoh's defection came as a result of him being satisfied working with All Japan in the inter-promotional events and dissatisfied with his home promotion. This was in part due to the former IWGP Heavyweight Champion's position on the card in New Japan, with a roster that was crowded at the time.

'Mutoh really enjoyed being in 2001 All Japan. He felt like they needed him. Mutoh needs to be in the main event. He can't be in the mid-card'.

One of the wrestlers Mutoh brought with him, Satoshi Kojima, was a rising star who had similarly found the political situation in New Japan stifling. As well as the usual slow rise to the top present in any Japanese promotion, New Japan Pro Wrestling was encountering some lean times of its own. Part of the issue was that New Japan's management were booking its talent in Mixed Martial Arts (MMA) bouts as part of Antonio Inoki's intent to make professional wrestling appear to be the dominant form of martial arts. This idea destroyed some wrestlers' marketability, as they so often entered MMA bouts against elite-level opponents without enough time to adequately prepare.

With Mutoh, Kojima, and Kashin no doubt re-evaluating their future in this context, the jump to All Japan allowed each man to play a role in the next stage of the company's rebuilding. For Mutoh and Kojima, this included becoming part of a new incarnation of the 'Four Pillars'. Under this proposal, All Japan would revolve around Mutoh, Kojima, Tenryu, and Kawada, the new focal points of the promotion[110].

For a variety of reasons, this idea did not last. While Mutoh embarked on a long run with the promotion that lasted all the way up to 2013, Genichiro Tenryu's tenure with All Japan Pro Wrestling ended in 2004. Tenryu fostered his own ambition of becoming All Japan president, but this agenda was stifled by Motoko Baba[111]. When the journeyman wrestler left once more, All Japan was in a far more stable position thanks to his contributions. Tenryu's presence had shifted the narrative away from the company's alleged pending demise and stabilised the Triple Crown Heavyweight Championship.

The other wrestler who may be considered All Japan's post-split Most Valuable Player is Toshiaki Kawada, whose decision to stay with the company proved to be life-saving. According to Fumi Saito, 'If Kawada had left, there was only one wrestler, Masa

Fuchi. All Japan would have gone down right away'.

Dave Meltzer agreed with this sentiment, naming Kawada as All Japan's Most Valuable Wrestler in his year-end awards for the year 2000: 'If you are going to list a Most Valuable Wrestler to their promotion over the past year, Kawada would win hands down. Basically, there would be no All Japan Pro Wrestling today, except possibly as a tiny indie drawing 200 fans per show, had Kawada joined his former high school classmate in the big jump.

'Kawada's staying was strong enough that the company was able to sell-out three straight Budokan Hall shows with a skeleton crew, have the inter-promotional feud with New Japan work well enough for a Tokyo Dome sell-out ,and one of the biggest matches in the history of the Japanese business with Kensuke Sasaki'[112].

Of course, Motoko Baba was the other figure who had ensured the company's survival. Moving All Japan from crisis to recovery no doubt took its toll on her, however, and she did not plan to stay with the company in the long term.

Baba briefly considered closing All Japan altogether in October 2002. This idea involved marking the thirtieth anniversary of Shohei Baba's promotion by bringing it to a dignified and definite close. Independently wealthy, Motoko Baba certainly did not need any money that the company might bring in. The Babas had previously made their fortune in Hawaii's real estate market. Except for, possibly, Vince McMahon, they were the richest promoters in professional wrestling. In 1990, when All Japan co-promoted a Tokyo Dome show with the WWF, wrestling insiders broadly understood Baba to be wealthier than McMahon[113]. Now in her sixties, Baba also did not feel the need to travel around Japan with the promotion that she owned.

Instead of selling to New Japan or closing the promotion, however, Baba's exit from professional wrestling took an entirely different route. A convincing pitch from an unexpected source saw arguably the most powerful woman in professional wrestling sell most of her stock and make her exit from an industry she had been deeply entrenched in for nearly three decades.

Motoko Baba's next step will be further explored in the closing chapter.

Conclusion to Chapter Five

Motoko Baba managed All Japan Pro Wrestling from the crisis phase to the post-crisis phase, working to reframe the company's situation from an ailing organisation that had suffered mass defections to the site of multiple returns and a previously unthinkable working relationship with New Japan Pro Wrestling.

Importantly, Baba used the 'golden hour' and acted quickly to bring these changes to fruition. With a number of exciting matchups taking place in All Japan, the promotion shored up its fortunes. Despite early expectations, All Japan sold out sizable arenas such as the Budokan and remained profitable into 2001[114]. Having made a number of key strategic moves to rescue the company, Baba was ready to move to another stage in her life.

Meanwhile, as All Japan emerged from a company-wide crisis, Mitsuharu Misawa's new promotion spent its early days going from strength to strength. Chapter Six will explore how Pro Wrestling NOAH handled their promotional launch, eventually coming to dominate Japan's pro wrestling industry.

CHAPTER SIX: PRO WRESTLING NOAH

All Japan Pro Wrestling spent much of 2000 and 2001 stabilising and working to turn their situation around, first with Genichiro Tenryu's return, then via a working relationship with previous nemesis New Japan Pro Wrestling. Meanwhile, Mitsuharu Misawa and his 'ark', full of wrestlers departing All Japan, found themselves the talk of the wrestling industry, with much of the attention on their first few shows.

As the name suggests, Pro Wrestling NOAH's founding myth is one that takes images and terms from the *Genesis* story of Noah's Ark.

A broad range of theologians believe that the *Genesis* account reworks older flood narratives to create a new story. In this version, there is a singular deity in keeping with Ancient Israel's monotheism, a God who grieves over the state of the world and later promises to never again allow such a catastrophic flood to happen. While Misawa's use of the story was not theological in its intent, as we will see, his new promotion in turn used Noah's Ark as part of its own story.

Hisame is a translator and professional wrestling fan who maintains a widely-read blog that seeks to contextualise Pro Wrestling NOAH for international fans who may otherwise miss some of the storyline nuances. In an early entry, she described the symbol of the ark and the significance that it held for Misawa and the wrestlers who had joined him in 2000: 'From its early days the Ark would be a symbol that everyone in Noah would go the same way together and pull together during times of crisis, like the crew of a ship in a storm. The offices and the dojo were set up in the Differ Ariake arena in Tokyo, and it would become home to NOAH for the next fifteen or sixteen years'[115].

As well as the majority of All Japan's native roster, three *gaijin* talent joined Misawa's journey to a new promotion: Vader, Scorpio, and Richard Aslinger (who wrestled as Richard Slinger). In an interview, Aslinger explained that he chose NOAH because of the high level of talent that joined the exodus. 'The reason I decided to go with NOAH is because that's where the top talent was. I was also offered the chance to come [back] to All Japan but the wise choice was NOAH in my view,' Aslinger said.

'Working for NOAH was a great experience. If I had not blown my ACL out, my career there would have had much greater potential. I loved being in the presence of a great bunch of guys such as Misawa-San, Ogawa-San, Kobashi-San, and so many others. It was certainly a different era in professionalism, the likes of which the world may never witness again'.

Getting on to the ark

In keeping with the ark theme, some of the promotion's tours were deemed 'Navigations' and the commentators for these shows were referred to as 'Navigators'.

Along with NOAH's biblical imagery, the new promotion's branding included green as its main colour. Misawa had admired German wrestler Horst Hoffman, who captured his imagination in Japan in the early 1970s, and whose signature colour was green. Misawa wore green ring attire in honour of Hoffman throughout his career, and featured it on his promotion's ring apron, logo, and lighting[116].

More than any thematic names or colour usage, Pro Wrestling NOAH represented Mitsuharu Misawa's opportunity to present wrestling the way that he wanted. During his presidency of All Japan Pro Wrestling, Misawa and Motoko Baba clashed over his ideas. Introducing pyrotechnics, video screens, and big stages were ideas that were deemed to be outside of the traditional wrestling presentation that Baba hoped to preserve in the wake of her husband's death[117][118]. Unencumbered by such organisational limitations, Misawa was free to introduce these modern elements to All Japan Pro Wrestling's traditional *Oudou* style.

Indeed, for all of the new means of presenting its product, Pro Wrestling NOAH retained much of the original style that had been a hallmark of All Japan in the 1990s and earlier. Hisame is a longtime NOAH fan and translator who runs the unofficial English NOAH blog *Puro Translations*. In an interview conducted for this book, she said that the promotion's contribution to the pro wrestling industry was one of preserving, what is called 'passivity' (i.e. the art of selling a move) and, as they called it, 'the fight with aesthetics' (wrestling as an art form) which comes from Giant Baba.

Hisame also pointed to another, less obvious part of NOAH's style as being directly lifted from Baba's vision of pro wrestling: 'Baba had a certain sound he wanted his wrestlers to make when taking moves, and he wouldn't let them debut until they could do it. If you listen very carefully, you can hear this sound in NOAH. It's hard to explain what it is, but if you listen, you will hear it.'

In other words, while NOAH introduced elements that Motoko Baba had gone out of her way to keep from introducing to All Japan before the split, Misawa's new venture has, ironically enough, served since to preserve traditions from years past.

Pro Wrestling NOAH showcased this mixture of old and new during their first shows in 2000. A number of wrestlers used these shows as an opportunity to debut new outfits. This was itself a demonstration of newfound freedom. As Fumi Saito recalled, Giant Baba had initiated a tradition in All Japan whereby wrestlers wore the same colours for their entire career.

'Once you had green trunks you had wear green trunks until the day you retired,' Saito said. 'When Pro Wrestling NOAH started, everyone changed their colours. Kobashi's neon orange became black and white'.

NOAH's first ever main event featured Jun Akiyama turning heel after he and Kobashi beat Misawa and Taue in a tag team main event. One of the stipulations was that the winners were scheduled to face one another in singles match the next night. After the match, Akiyama attacked Kobashi with a back suplex. The message could not be clearer: he was not going to take a back seat in the new promotion and was now set for another main event.

Sure enough, NOAH's second show saw Akiyama defeat Kobashi, cementing himself as one of the new promotion's top stars, on the same level as those who he had trailed in All Japan. This was also bold statement from Pro Wrestling NOAH on how their booking approach, with Misawa booking the promotion's biggest stars in ways that were different to their prior incarnations. The wrestling itself matched the prior expectations placed on King's Road, but Misawa was free to depart from Baba's strictures as he deemed necessary.

According to Saito, for many wrestlers, Pro Wrestling NOAH represented a new start, a potential 'utopia' that they escaped to. This was not universally the case, however. Kakihara was the first wrestler to defect from NOAH back to All Japan, after only one match with the former, and only two months after the initial exodus.

Takao Omori is another wrestler for whom the green mat did not represent greener pastures. Omori and Misawa did not get along, and their relationship was further inflamed when Omori received an outside booking in the United States for Harley Race's World League Wrestling promotion. Misawa contended that this appearance was not authorised, and the resulting disagreement saw Omori leave Pro Wrestling NOAH in 2002. After stints in Zero One and Hustle, he re-joined All Japan in April 2004 in time for that year's Champion Carnival tournament.

For better or worse, NOAH was Misawa's company.

This was also evident when he abandoned the isolationism of late 1990s All Japan and opted to work extensively with other wrestling organisations. Over time, he set up working relationships with Germany's WXW, Ring of Honor in America, and several promotions in Mexico, where Misawa had worked earlier in his career[119].

Furthering its own identity meant NOAH needed to introduce its own championships, and the promotion started this process with a tournament to crown the inaugural Global Honoured Crown (GHC) Heavyweight Champion. As is so often the case with pro wrestling promotors who are also active, Misawa gave himself the task of becoming the first champion, defeating Yoshihiro Takayama in a tournament final on 15 April 2001.

Far from being any kind of vanity reign, however, this served the purpose of putting NOAH's world title on its most established star, heating the belt up before placing it on a new star. As Saito put it, 'You have to beat someone to become someone. It was necessary [for Misawa] to become inaugural champion'.

Indeed, Misawa put Jun Akiyama over for the GHC Heavyweight title on 27 July 2001. After holding the title for nearly a year, Akiyama dropped the belt to Yoshinari Ogawa, making another new star in the process. The GHC Junior Heavyweight Championship was decided via a month-long tournament, with Yoshinobu Kanemaru besting Juventud Guerrera on 24 June 2001. Tag team championships followed, with a tournament final on 19 October 2001 crowning the team of Vader and Scorpio, two of the *gaijin* talents who had joined the Misawa exodus. Nearly two years later, NOAH introduced a version of the tag team championships for junior heavyweights, when KENTA and Marufuji became the inaugural champions after winning a tournament.

As well as establishing its own championships, NOAH needed to further distinguish itself from its All Japan roots by introducing its own home-grown stars. From 2001 to 2003, the NOAH dojo produced a number of prospects that went on to greater stardom, within the promotion and beyond. Entering the dojo after its gruelling tryout process, Kotaro Suzuki became one of the world's highest-regarded junior heavyweights.

Some two years later, Go Shiozaki entered the dojo, going on to become the only one in his class to graduate and becoming the youngest member of the NOAH roster. Eddie Edwards is one of the few foreign talents to graduate from the dojo[120]. Years after graduating, Edwards won the GHC Heavyweight Championship, becoming the first *gaijin* to do so. In a post-victory press conference, Edwards, who at that point worked for the American promotion Impact Wrestling, confirmed that he still considered himself a product of the NOAH dojo. 'I am an Impact wrestler, but I am also a NOAH wrestler,' Edwards said[121].

As this quote suggests, Pro Wrestling NOAH successfully trained its own home-grown talents and eventually made them big stars. This, however, was a slow process and there was still some way to go for NOAH when it came to building their future. For the first three years of the title's existence, the GHC Heavyweight Championship was held by talent that made their names in All Japan Pro Wrestling.

The slow build to make new stars eventually became a problem for the company, but, for the first few years of its existence, NOAH's hard-hitting use of the traditional King's Road in-ring style combined with a newer presentation style proved irresistible for many fans. Tickets for the promotion's first two shows sold out within twenty minutes.

While the promotion initially booked out mid-sized arenas, the early sell-outs were a harbinger of bigger success to come, as NOAH eventually overtook All Japan and New Japan in 2004/05 to become the highest earning *puroresu* promotion. Indeed, at the promotion's height, Misawa refused to book the Ryōgoku Sumo Hall (capacity 11,098) as he considered the arena too small[122].

At first glance, NOAH's growth and dominance can

be read as Misawa's vindication: proof positive that the deposed All Japan president was right to lead the majority of the roster out the door and to start up a promotion where he could implement his vision for professional wrestling.

A more careful reading of the numbers, however, reveals that while Misawa could take satisfaction from such rapid growth in a short time, NOAH overtook other companies at a time when Japan's professional wrestling was declining in overall popularity. As Chris Charlton put it, 'Truly, while NOAH's slice of the wrestling pie was getting larger and larger, the problem was that the dish itself continued to shrink'[123]. Nonetheless, when Pro Wrestling NOAH hit its peak, it did so in style, going so far as to promote multiple shows in the Tokyo Dome.

Misawa sought Motoko Baba's public blessing for his new endeavour prior to the 28 May 2000 press conference announcing his resignation. When Baba turned this down, it set the tone for the relationship between the two companies over the next few years. As long as All Japan remained under Baba's ownership, there was bad blood between the two companies, which gave way to the occasional petty gestures. While Baba remained All Japan's majority owner, she went so far as to erase Misawa's matches and name from any future DVD releases, regardless of what this might cost the company[124].

Furthermore, Baba remained so incensed over the Misawa-led exodus that she banned anyone associated with it from appearing at All Japan's memorial events for her late husband. Misawa responded in kind.

On 14 April 2002, NOAH sponsored Kodo Fuyuki's retirement show, a common occurrence in Japanese wrestling that traditionally features wrestlers from multiple promotions wrestling, appearing in non-wrestling roles, and generally paying their respects to the performer marking the end of their active time in the ring.

The relationship between All Japan and NOAH was so strained at the time that Misawa sent Yoshinari Ogawa to collect Genichiro Tenryu by car. This meant the GHC Heavyweight champion picked up the Triple Crown Champion[125].

Conclusion to Chapter Six

Pro Wrestling NOAH's formation in 2000 was a source of consternation for All Japan Pro Wrestling, instantly regarded by Motoko Baba as an act of betrayal. Misawa and his new company nonetheless took All Japan Pro Wrestling's traditional King's Road style with them and retained key elements, all the while implementing a new presentation style with elements such as pyro, new looks for the roster, and elaborate staging.

Finding early success, the company managed to build a fanbase and capitalise on attention generated through its controversial beginnings. As NOAH grew, and Baba remained in All Japan, there was still bad blood between the two. The possibility of any forgiveness, reconciliation, or any amiable working relationship seemed to be remote, despite their shared heritage and wrestling style.

As we will see, however, this was all set to change, as the Misawa/Baba story found its unexpected conclusion.

BABA AND MISAWA: A CODA

The relationship between All Japan Pro Wrestling and Pro Wrestling NOAH remained frosty during the early days of the post-split era.

Motoko Baba guided the company started by her late husband, making many quick and strategic decisions to manage and mitigate All Japan's crisis, eventually creating some buzz for the ailing brand by bringing in two unexpected wrestlers in Genichiro Tenryu and Keiji Mutoh.

While willing to work with New Japan, and going so far as to bring Genichiro Tenryu back, Baba was more unforgiving towards those involved in Misawa's new venture.

Even as NOAH's early days promised so much by way of growth, providing Misawa with her blessing to leave proved to be too much for Motoko Baba to contemplate. Further, she went so far as to ensure that no one from the NOAH roster was invited to the first Giant Baba memorial show in 2001.

Between 2000 and 2002, the prospect of any kind of working agreement between the two companies promoting the King's Road/*Oudou* style seemed to be remote at best.

The bitterness was not confined to one side, with Misawa occasionally demonstrating a lack of patience as regarded All Japan as an organisation, his refusal to pay for a car to pick up the Triple Crown Champion for Fuyuki's retirement show a somewhat amusing example of his exasperation.

Thankfully the acrimony between the two companies did not last, and an event previously considered unthinkable eventually happened. First, however, there were some key changes to All Japan Pro Wrestling.

Meet the new boss

According to Fumi Saito, Keiji Mutoh had long planned to work his way into the organisation's presidency. The idea, he said, came from a close friend of Mutoh's who happened to be a professional politician.

Hioshi Hase and Keiji Mutoh fought in one of the bloodiest matches in pro wrestling history, with the latter playing his role of The Great Muta. The match was so violent that pro wrestling writers later invoked the 'Muta scale' to describe particularly bloody matches.

In true professional wrestling fashion, the two became good friends after working together and remained in contact, even after Hase jumped to All Japan and was elected to the Japanese Diet. According to Fumi Saito, Hase told Mutoh, 'Why don't you actually legitimately resign from New Japan and sign a contract with All Japan and…you can [eventually] become president.'

'Keiji Mutoh came in and decided to take over. Mrs Baba trusted Mutoh's idea right away'.

Hiroshi Hase brokered a deal between the two parties, and in September 2002, Mutoh officially became All Japan's president[126]. Motoko Baba sold the majority of her stock in the company to a group of financial backers and handed control over to Keiji Mutoh. Mutoh's first official act as president was to announce a new broadcast deal between All Japan and Fuji TV [127]. Motoko Baba was no longer involved in All Japan's day-to-day business. It was the end of an era.

Ironically enough, Mutoh's presidency modernised All Japan's presentation and changing the names of some of the annual shows and tours. While the Champion Carnival and World's Strongest Tag Determination League remained, Mutoh renamed the likes of the Summer Action Series, rebranding and replacing tours that All Japan fans had previously anticipated all year in their calendars.

The Mutoh era of All Japan is a fascinating one, however it falls outside the scope of the book at hand, focused as it is on the All Japan split, the formation of NOAH, and how the former survived. As well as acting as a clear end point for our story however, Mutoh's ascendency also provides a coda to the events of 2000 to 2002.

A previously unthinkable return

Despite belonging to two rival companies during the height of the 1990s, Keiji Mutoh and Mitsuharu Misawa were always cordial with one another. In 1999, when Misawa became All Japan president, Mutoh, then with New Japan, crossed the corporate divide to present him with flowers (a gift shared between businesspeople during important occasions such as a promotion or retirement).

In 2002, Mutoh's ascendency, combined with Motoko Baba's exit, removed the barrier between Misawa and his former company. Cooperation between All Japan and Pro Wrestling NOAH had become possible at long last.

In 2004, All Japan and NOAH embarked on a new working relationship. This was a huge departure from the acrimony of the year 2000 that had led one company to form while the other struggled to stay afloat.

On 10 July 2004, Taiyō Kea and Keiji Mutoh teamed to take on Misawa and Yoshinari Ogawa for the GHC Tag Team Championships during one of NOAH's Tokyo Dome shows, Departure. The show also featured former All Japan veterans Kenta Kobashi and Jun Akiyama in the main event, as well as cooperation from New Japan.

Later in July, a previously unthinkable return took place. Misawa faced Satoshi Kojima in the semi-main event of All Japan Pro Wrestling's *Battle Banquet* show on 18 July 2004. In many ways, the match signalled an end to old hostilities. As the ring announcer introduced Misawa, he indicated that the man in the long emerald tights represented Pro Wrestling NOAH while on his old stomping grounds. The two were in perfect harmony.

It was a physical match in the King's Road style. Over the course of about thirty minutes, Misawa gave Kojima the majority of the offense, and went as far as allowing Kojima to kick out of his Emerald Frosion finishing move. It was Misawa whose hand was raised at the end of the night, which may have been a political move to keep Pro Wrestling NOAH happy at an early point in the working relationship. However, Misawa had typically worked to ensure that his opponent looked better in defeat than he did going into the match.

On 31 October 2004, Misawa returned once more to team with Mutoh in a tag team match against Hiroshi Hase and Kesuke Sasaki in a pay per view main event that commemorated Mutoh's twentieth anniversary as a professional wrestler. In what was already a foregone conclusion, Misawa and Mutoh beat Hiroshi Hase and Kensuke Sasaki.

Another reunion took place the following year, this time on the other side of the boundary created by the split. By 2005, Toshiaki Kawada was a freelancer, wrestling matches in All Japan, New Japan, and Hustle. The journeyman made an unexpected stop in Pro Wrestling NOAH with one purpose: to challenge his old rival to a final match that had seemed impossible years before.

On 18 July 2005, Misawa and Kawada met in the main event of a Tokyo Dome show. They were older and beat up from years of the King's Road style, but the two wrestlers did not hesitate to pull out their biggest, most dangerous, moves. Misawa dropped Kawada on his head and shoulders with his Tiger Driver '91. Kawada hit Misawa with his equally dangerous *ganso* bomb. The match, however, ended with a somewhat anticlimactic elbow strike from Misawa, who later remarked, 'In the end, that was all it took'[128].

Both men left the Tokyo Dome encounter open to the possibility of a rematch. However, it was the last time Mitsuharu Misawa wrestled his old high school friend. Tragedy struck four years later in Hiroshima.

Final departure

In 2009, Misawa was sore and exhausted. With his retirement pushed back multiple times, Mitsuharu Misawa remained in the green ring in order to pass the torch. NOAH had previously tried unsuccessfully to make new stars, with the likes of Rikio floundering. The latest plan was to promote Go Shiozaki by teaming him with Misawa. After they won the 2009 Global Tag League, Misawa and Shiozaki had a 13 June match against the GHC Tag Team Champions, Akitoshi Saito and Bison Smith.

During the match, Saito picked Misawa up for a back suplex, which he apparently hit properly so as to not injure his opponent. After years of abuse and heavy bumps, however, Misawa's body gave out. After telling the referee that he could not move, he failed to get back up.

While members of the crowd wept, wrestlers were heard calling on Misawa to get to his feet. American wrestler Chris Hero was at ringside after Misawa took the dreadful bump.

He later recalled feeling anxiety. 'The moment at ringside felt like an eternity,' Hero said. 'Never, in my life, have I wanted the fighting spirit to jump into someone's being more than I wanted it tonight,' he continued. 'The fans chanted Misawa, Misawa, Misawa. They wanted their Hero to get up so fucking bad. Just get up. Come on! You're too tough for this. Too strong. I grabbed his boots and held onto them 'til they took him away'[129].

A doctor who happened to be in attendance at the show checked on Misawa and tried to revive him. EMTs rushed to the ring and carried him out on a stretcher. Misawa was taken to Hiroshima College Hospital. At 10:10pm, he was pronounced dead.

The Misawa family invoked a Japanese law to keep the cause of death quiet. However, police later disclosed that the specific injury was the separation of the first and second cervical vertebrae (*atlantoaxial dislocation*).

Several wrestlers previously retired in order to avoid the condition that caused Misawa's death. 'Stone Cold' Steve Austin and Diamond Dallas Page are two famous western wrestlers who retired rather than face the risk to their necks that came with further bumps[130].

That Misawa was never diagnosed as being at risk is likely the result of his perceived necessity to gut it out through pain and the demands of carrying his company, so as to ensure that NOAH survived. As Richard Aslinger put it, 'Misawa-San...had so much love for the business and the fans he literally gave his life in the ring'.

Misawa's family held a private funeral on 18 June, which some 100 people attended[131]. Meanwhile, people made their way to NOAH's Tokyo offices to leave flowers. NOAH's show the next day was sold out, as fans made their way out to pay their respects to the man who had led the exodus from All Japan Pro Wrestling.

Misawa's death led to an outpouring of grief and condolences from across the wrestling world. For NOAH, this meant that fans continued to express their support for the fallen company founder the day after the accident occurred: 'All Misawa merchandise that they had brought to last the entire tour sold out before the show started.

'They opened the show with a ten count for Misawa, as shows did all over the world on that day (of major promotions running around the world the next day, only WWE and TNA failed to acknowledge it at their house shows, although both did post messages on their web site. WWE did not acknowledge it during Raw, but C.M. Punk did manage to sneak a mention in, writing his name in huge letters on the tape on his wrists and forearms). They played his music one last time and fans chanted his name'[132].

NOAH later held a public ceremony to honour

Misawa. While they anticipated some 5,000 people, more than 26,000 lined up to pay their respects[133], the second biggest attendance at a Japanese athlete's funeral, behind Giant Baba's[134].

Misawa's death had a profound impact on Pro Wrestling NOAH and the Japanese wrestling industry at large.

One area that was clearly affected was NOAH's fanbase. As Fumi Saito explained, 'In the back of your mind, this is wrestling.... when it's over they have to be safe. That's why this Misawa thing…we can never get over it. You don't want your hero to die in the ring.'

For some fans, the impact of the NOAH founder's death was such that they gave up on the product altogether.

'A lot of people walked away from wrestling that night,' Saito said. 'You [had] to wait another seven or eight years for another generation [of fans to emerge]'.

The wrestlers themselves were deeply affected by Misawa's passing, their lives and careers forever altered. While Toshiaki Kawada never officially retired, the event diminished his passion for wrestling and led to him stay away from the ring.

Another group that became more cautious were wrestling companies themselves. After Kenta Kobashi suffered a number of worrying injuries,

NOAH management felt compelled to keep him away from the ring. On 3 December 2012, they released him from his contract. While they did not mention Misawa's death as the impetus, it is likely to have played some role in informing the controversial business decision.

NOAH's decision to part ways with Kobashi had other consequences for the promotion. In a display of protest and solidarity with Kobashi, Jun Akiyama, Atsushi Aoki, Go Shiozaki, Kotaro Suzuki, and Yoshinobu Kanemaru gave notice that they intended to leave once their contracts were up at the end of the year. In a reversal of the year 2000 split, these five wrestlers defected to All Japan, making their debut for the company on 26 January 2013[135]. Together, this group of freelancers formed the third incarnation of the Burning stable. The Burning faction members all signed new contracts with the promotion in June 2013, marking their return to a promotion that they had previously exited in controversial fashion.

There is unfortunately no evidence of there ever being forgiveness or reconciliation between Motoko Baba and Mitsuharu Misawa before Misawa's untimely death. According to Saito, 'Mrs Baba was stubborn enough, that even if she forgave someone in her heart, she wouldn't tell them'.

Even in the absence of any public forgiveness, Baba was clearly moved by Misawa's passing enough to suggest that when she received the phone call, she knew something had happened to him[136]. In what might be considered a final display of deference, Baba attended Misawa's private funeral[137].

Motoko Baba herself passed away nine years later, on 14 April 2018. She was seventy-eight. Since selling her stock to Mutoh in 2002, Baba largely left professional wrestling behind, returning only briefly to promote her own produce show in 2005 and to act as a figurehead for All Japan in June 2014.

When Baba became ill, she displayed her fighting spirit until the end. On one occasion, doctors told her that she had mere weeks to live. Baba confounded them when she made a full recovery. In keeping with Japanese privacy traditions, word of Baba's passing did not reach media outlets until eight days later[138].

On 25 April 2018, All Japan started their show at Korakuen Hall with a ten-count ceremony for Motoko Baba and the recently departed Bruno Sammartino, with Akiyama holding Baba's photo and Fuchi holding Sammartino's. Pro Wrestling NOAH featured a similar tribute with some of the wrestlers who were previously part of All Japan, including Naomichi Marufuji.

That same month, from 7 to 20 April, Marufuji participated in All Japan's annual Champion Carnival.

This caused some concern in his home promotion as Marufuji was also booked for NOAH's own gruelling league tournament, the Global League[139]. On 25 April, Marufuji met fellow B block member Jun Akiyama. This match had much significance for all of the subjects of this book. A hard hitting, well-paced affair, there was much going on below the surface.

As Hisame writes: 'On 25 April 2018, after five years, Naomichi Marufuji and Jun Akiyama met in the ring. They had an epic battle. In this match everything came out, the difficult years, the dark past, the resentment, the bitterness, the lid blew off and the miasma scattered as they hit each other (the bruises could be seen the next day very clearly). Fans of both NOAH and All Japan were in tears as it was emotional.

'Like the ghosts of Taira clan watching Hoichi The Earless play "The Tale of The Heike", they saw it all; the shared past of Misawa and Kawada, Baba, Mokoto, Jumbo Tsuruta and the old guard, then the upturning of Puro and the new way it was taken in the new century, the return of Kobashi and the Burning stable made up of those who walked out of NOAH, all of it.'

'At the end of it, the demons exorcised, the past was laid finally to rest by a simple gesture of a fist bump between the two. Naomichi Marufuji would later call this match a "purification battle"'[140].

More than any pre-determined finish, the Champion Carnival bout between Akiyama and Marufuji was emblematic of the real-world clash between All Japan and NOAH, starting with hostility and ending with respect between competitors.

More tangibly, Marufuji versus Akiyama was the kind of match that can happen when wrestling promotions put past differences aside and focus on giving fans the kind of product they want. It embodied how All Japan and NOAH persevered through hard times, without needing to be constrained by the past bad blood between Misawa and Baba.

In considering all of these events, the question has to be asked: Could All Japan's split in the year 2000 have been avoided with more open communication between Motoko Baba and Mitsuharu Misawa?

No, according to Fumi Saito. 'I don't think it was avoidable,' he said. 'The split had to come'.

In part, Saito believes that the nature of the 'family feud' between Misawa and Motoko Baba combined with irreconcilable differences in vision to make the split inevitable.

This, he said, was due to Motoko Baba still viewing Misawa as she did when he was her husband's young protégé, while Misawa felt the need to 'leave home' so as to be able to make his own mark on the professional wrestling industry.

Another question that sometimes comes to wrestling fans' mind when discussing the split is whether or not the passage of time and changes to the wrestling landscape mean that All Japan Pro Wrestling and Pro Wrestling NOAH might reunify and form one singular great wrestling company?

As Hisame observed, however, such a unification would fly in the face of Misawa and Baba's own wishes for their respective companies: Misawa struck out on his own to create Pro Wrestling NOAH, never expecting the support he received. Motoko Baba fought hard to keep alive the company her husband formed. Furthermore, the sheer number of wrestlers now working for each company means such a merger might be difficult from a practical standpoint[141].

Adding to this is the complications that the companies' corporate structures now pose. All Japan continues to run as its own entity. On the other hand, in 2020, Pro Wrestling NOAH was purchased by CyberFight, an IT company that added the promotion to DDT and Tokyo Joshi Pro Wrestling. Barring the unlikely possibility of an acquisition, All Japan and NOAH will remain separate entities.

Ganbaru Conclusion

Through its interviews and analysis, *Ganbaru* has sought to illustrate how All Japan Pro Wrestling survived the 2000 'split' that led to the creation of Pro Wrestling NOAH.

A major theme that stands out is that the split was something of a family division that took place during a time of grief as Mitsuharu Misawa clashed with Motoko Baba after the death of a man who was a father figure to him. Fumi Saito likened these events to a Shakespearian story involving a royal family: a king passing away, a queen who seeks to maintain order, and a deposed new king who seeks to return the kingdom to former glory.

In keeping with this theme, all of the participants in the split are unique and flawed characters. *Ganbaru* has sought to explore them in all of this complexity. Like many of Shakespeare's plots, the story ended with so much tragedy for all involved.

Another major theme that runs throughout this book is that of resilience, as All Japan Pro Wrestling survived despite early predictions it would fold. The company went on to experience lean times, downsizing both its roster and the arenas it ran in as the wrestling industry struggled as a whole. Again, however, All Japan fought through these financial strains (and others that make fertile ground for another book).

In more recent times, All Japan has shown signs of turning the corner. The promotion is currently working to create new stars, under the leadership of its young ace Kento Miyahara and former Triple Crown Heavyweight Champion Jake Lee. These wrestlers' in-ring approach might be deemed 'new King's Road', a physical style that is similar to that of the 1990s, but with a more measured approach to bumps and fewer dangerous head-dropping moves.

This product appears to be supported by an equally solid business plan. During the COVID-19 pandemic, the company announced that they had successfully shifted to a new and unique financial tactic. Investing in one of the few films released in Japanese cinemas in 2020 paid off[142]. In 2020, when many other wrestling leagues folded (Wrestle-1) or struggled to survive (Zero One and Big Japan Pro Wrestling), All Japan Pro Wrestling made a slight profit at the end of the year. This money was clearly put into improving its production values, with the pre-match videos and in ring camera work visibly improving.

In 2022, All Japan Pro Wrestling celebrates the fiftieth anniversary of its first show. In interviews, All Japan executive Kohei Suwama hinted that the company will do something big to celebrate[143].

With New Japan Pro Wrestling celebrating their own fiftieth anniversary in the same year, there are rumblings at the time of writing that the two companies may collaborate again (although nothing has yet been announced).

In a recent interview, Suwama indicated that he aims to eventually returning to bigger arenas, such as the Ryogoku Sumo Hall, Nippon Budokan, and the Tokyo Dome [144]. More recently, the promotion announced that it will run its first Budokan show in eighteen years this September.

All Japan has changed over the years, to the point where, as Fumi Saito put it, 'Today's All Japan isn't Baba's All Japan.' However, he noted that the company still uses the old logo and championships, and still runs the Baba-era tournaments such as the Champion Carnival and World's Strongest Tag League.

To keep the promotion running into the future, All Japan needs to continue creating new stars, and the promotion's dojo continues to train and produce younger talent.

Recent graduate and former World Junior Heavyweight Champion Francisco Akira has suggested that, from what he understands of company tradition, the current dojo is closely modelled after Giant Baba's original vision for how to train professional wrestlers. A number of promising rookies recently started their All Japan careers, including the Saito brothers and Ryoma Tsukamoto.

All of this is a far cry from that fateful day in 2000 when the company was declared, 'all but dead'[145]. All Japan Pro Wrestling lives on, and will continue to fight through hard times, perhaps one day reclaiming its former glory as Japan's top professional wrestling organisation.

[1] Alt, 2020
[2] Blassie, 2003: 94
[3] Charlton, 2015: 10
[4] Charlton, 2015: 8
[5] Hornbaker, 2006, Chapter 17, para. 18
[6] Meltzer, 2018
[7] Hansen, 2014, Chapter 14, 126
[8] Podgorski, 2020
[9] Senshu Shōkai podcast, 2020

[11] Hansen, 2014, Chapter 14, paragraph 43
[12] Hansen, 2014, Chapter 14, paragraph 38
[13] Hansen, 2014, Chapter 16, paragraphs 26 and 27
[14] Foley, 1999: 251
[15] Foley, 1999: 257
[16] Blassie, 2013: 134
[17] Hisame, 2018a
[18] Meltzer, 2018
[19] Hansen, 2014, Chapter 16, paragraph 18
[20] Foley, 1999: 251
[21] Meltzer, 2015
[22] Saito on Suwama's Station podcast, 2020
[23] Ichinose, 2015, cited in Charlton, 2018: 180
[24] Charlton, 2018: 119

[25] Podgorski, 2020
[26] Podgorski, 2020
[27] Charlton, 2018: 119
[28] Meltzer, 2000b
[29] Wada, 2004, cited in Charlton, 2018: 119
[30] Meltzer, 2009
[31] Podorski, 2020
[32] Hansen, 2014: Chapter 14, paragraph 77
[33] Podgorski, 2017
[34] Schneider, 2021: 232
[35] Charlton, 2018: 119
[36] Suwama's Station podcast, 2021
[37] Hisame, 2018a
[38] Charlton, 2018
[39] Senshu Shōkai podcast, 2020
[40] Charlton, 2018: 145
[41] The Four Pillars, 2021b
[42] Hansen, 2014, Chapter 15, paragraph 74
[43] Charlton, 2018
[44] Boulding, 2000
[45] Funk in Hansen, 2014, Foreword, paragraph 9
[46] Hart, 2007: 89
[47] Suwama's Station podcast, 2021
[48] Suwama's Station podcast, 2021
[49] Charlton, 2018: 27
[50] Suwama's Station podcast, 2021

[51] Charlton, 2018: 27-28
[52] Hansen, 2014, Chapter 20, Paragraph 24
[53] Hansen, 2014, Chapter 20, Paragraph 26
[54] Meltzer, as quoted in Charlton, 2018: 28
[55] Pacific Rim Podcast, 2020
[56] Asano, 1999, cited in Charlton, 2018: 41
[57] Yamamoto, 2010, cited in Charlton, 2018: 83
[58] Asano, 1999, cited in Charlton, 2018: 46
[59] Huseney & Eisener, 2021
[60] Suwama's Station, 2020b
[61] Meltzer, 2000
[62] Meltzer, 2018
[63] Hansen, 2014: Chapter 17, paragraph 5
[64] Charlton, 2018: 131
[65] The Four Pillars, 2021
[66] Senshu Shōkai podcast, 2020
[67] Meltzer, 2000a
[68] Ross, 2018: 14
[69] Meltzer, 2000
[70] Hisame, 2018a
[71] Meltzer, 2000b
[72] Meltzer, 2018
[73] Ross, 2020: 47
[74] Misawa/Suzuki, 2000, cited in Charlton, 2018: 145
[75] Charlton, 2018: 131

[76] Charlton, 2018: 132
[77] Charlton, 2018: 133
[78] Hisame, 2018a
[79] Meltzer, 2019
[80] Suwama's Station podcast, 2021
[81] Hansen, 2014: Chapter 9, Paragraph 12
[82] Hisame, 2018a
[83] Meltzer, 2000c
[84] Hisame, 2018b
[85] Molinaro, 2000
[86] Senshu Shōkai podcast, 2020
[87] Meltzer, 2000
[88] Suwama's Station podcast, 2021
[89] Hisame, 2018b
[90] Molinaro, 2000
[91] IGN Staff, 2000
[92] Molinaro, 2000
[93] Marui, 2010, cited in Charlton, 2018: 146
[94] Hansen, 2014, Chapter 20, paragraph 24
[95] Suwama's Station podcast, 2020
[96] Wada, 2004, cited in Charlton, 2018: 145
[97] Garcia, 2017: 38
[98] Meltzer, 2000c
[99] Meltzer, 2000d
[100] Charlton, 2018: 30
[101] Charlton, 2018: 146

[102] Meltzer, 2000e
[103] Meltzer, 2000b
[104] Meltzer, 2000b
[105] Hansen, 2014, Chapter 27, paragraph 4
[106] Hansen, 2014, Chapter 27, paragraph 15
[107] Meltzer, 2001
[108] Hansen, 2014, Chapter 27, paragraph 18
[109] Suwama's Station, 2021
[110] Week of Lariat podcast, 2020
[111] Suwama's Station podcast, 2021
[112] Meltzer, 2001
[113] Meltzer, 2018
[114] Meltzer, 2018
[115] Hisame, 2018a
[116] Hisame, 2018a
[117] Meltzer 2000
[118] Marui, 2010, cited in Charlton, 2018: 145
[119] Hisame, 2018a
[120] Hisame, 2018a
[121] Hisame, 2018c
[122] Senshu Shōkai podcast, 2020
[123] Charlton, 2018: 203
[124] Hisame, 2018a
[125] The Four Pillars, 2020
[126] Meltzer, 2018
[127] Meltzer, 2002

[128] Charlton, 2018: 215
[129] Podgorski, 2017
[130] Meltzer, 2009a
[131] Nikkan Sports, 2009b
[132] Meltzer, 2009b
[133] Nikkan Sports, 2009a
[134] Meltzer, 2009c
[135] Senshu Shōkai podcast, 2020
[136] Hisame, 2018b
[137] Nikkan Sports, 2009b
[138] Meltzer, 2018
[139] Senshu Shōkai podcast, 2020
[140] Hisame, 2018
[141] Pacific Rim Podcast, 2021
[142] Yahoo News Japan, 2020
[143] Daly, 2021
[144] Daly, 2021
[145] IGN Staff, 2000
[146] Eastern Lariat Podcast, 2021

ADDENDUM: FORGOTTEN GEMS

Having seen how All Japan survived the cataclysmic events of the 2000 split that created Pro Wrestling NOAH, we turn now to some additional material beyond our main narrative. This additional chapter looks at some of the classic matches that All Japan Pro Wrestling produced during the years 2000 to 2002.

Due to the story surrounding the split itself and the popularity of Pro Wrestling NOAH as a new product, many of these bouts have been neglected in present day discussions about the best matches that the company produced.

Further, these matches' availability was affected by shifts in All Japan's television presence. The promotion's streaming service, AJPW TV, does not feature many of the shows produced at the time due to complications regarding who owns the footage.

The following matches are forgotten classics that are worth watching, matches that were well received at the time but are now all-too overlooked in fan discourse, or bouts that feature historical significance that cannot be ignored.

Some of these matches are key to the story surrounding the 2000 All Japan split, while others are worth watching without that particular context in mind. These matches all take place during *Ganbaru*'s 2000 to 2002 timeframe.

Modern All Japan has many other subsequent matches that could also be considered underrated (Kawada's Triple Crown run from 2003 to 2005 produced many examples) and this list is presented as a provisional jumping on point for anyone that has yet to consider some of the classics that followed the split.

These matches are all strong bouts that viewers can appreciate without knowing any of the backstory; however knowing some of the context that surrounded them makes for a far more enjoyable experience. As such, the following section provides some of the backstory going into the match in question, an overview of the action, and some commentary as to why each match is truly a forgotten classic worthy of being 'rediscovered'.

Toshiaki Kawada vs Kensuke Sasaki, 9 October 2000, Tokyo Dome

This historic match between the IWGP Heavyweight Champion and the All Japan ace was the main event of New Japan Pro Wrestling's *Do Judge* in the Tokyo Dome.

While this match garnered quite the critical and fan response at the time, it is not brought up nearly as often as some of Kawada's other great matches.

Kawada vs Sasaki is the first to take place between the two promotions as part of their new feud, a factor that gave it a special mystique. The match itself is a physical brawl, with a lot of stiff shots and a loud crowd.

This match was a critical and financial success, with a record live gate for the time. The angle that follows the match sets up a number of matches afterwards and led to a rematch between the two at New Japan's Tokyo Dome show on 4 January 2001.

While Kawada and Sasaki's second bout is widely considered not quite as good as their original meeting, it is still also worth tracking down and watching, and is noteworthy as a rare rematch that took place in the same arena as the first.

While this is the main event of a New Japan show, rather than an All Japan card, the match's significance to the latter cannot be understated. Out of the matches on this list, it is one of the easiest to find, as it is available in full (sans entrances) on New Japan Pro Wrestling's streaming service, New Japan World.

Toshiaki Kawada vs Genichiro Tenryu, Triple Crown Heavyweight Championship, 28 October 2000, Nippon Budokan

Less than a month after his classic Tokyo Dome match with Kensuke Sasaki, Kawada was back in the main event. This time, he faced his former Revolution stablemate and tag team partner, Genichiro Tenryu.

The match also stands out for historic reasons, as it well and truly cemented Tenryu's return, a move that was Motoko Baba's ace in the hole when it came to All Japan's post-split recovery. More tangibly, the match also settled the question of who might replace Kenta Kobashi as the Triple Crown Heavyweight Champion.

At the time, the allure of seeing this match was enough to sell out the Nippon Budokan, making it a necessary shot in the arm for a promotion still overcoming the loss of most of its roster. As well as setting up the first post-split champion, this match stood as an historic bout between mentor (Tenryu) and protégé (Kawada). In this regard, it is interesting to see Kawada and Tenryu facing off in a match where their offence is quite similar, trading chops, stiff kicks, lariats, and power bombs. Considering that both men were quite beat up by this point in their careers, it is an impressive display.

The match is only the second singles bout between the two, with the first taking place in 1989 when Kawada was a much more inexperienced competitor. Taking place in front of a loud crowd who were heavily invested in both participants, the audience reactions further elevated the bout.

The story here is one of Kawada surprising Tenryu, who reacts with shock at some of Dangerous K's early chops and kicks, selling for him before making his patented grumpy comeback. For his part, Kawada displays the smart selling that is something of his trademark, indicating frustration at several points that he cannot hide his pain from his former mentor.

While Kawada vs Tenryu was later overshadowed

by subsequent title matches, it had an important role to play in re-establishing the Triple Crown and getting All Japan back on track to a point where they could promote future title matches. The match received four stars from the *Wrestling Observer* newsletter's review but may deserve an even higher rating due to its sheer physicality and the crowd response.

Masanobu Fuchi and Toshiaki Kawada vs. Takashi Iizuka and Yuji Nagata, 14 December 2000

While this match took place on a New Japan Pro Wrestling card, the ominously named the Second Judgement, the bout's importance to All Japan as part of the inter-promotional rivalry ensures that it belongs on this list.

This match saw the last two permanent native members of the pre-split All Japan roster go up against two New Japan stalwarts. It is also worth watching to see both Fuchi and Iizuka in a match where they play roles that more recent fans may not have previously seen them in. Fuchi, now beloved by fans as a long-term member of All Japan's roster, played the role of an invading heel.

For his part Iizuka, who contemporary fans largely know as a wild and deranged member of Suzuki-gun, excelled in this match as the face in peril, selling for the heel team and building anticipation for a tag. The match was heated and violent, with a hot crowd that was into everything that the wrestlers did. The workers involved all had clearly defined roles that they played to perfection.

Occurring during a year which produced a number of classic matches (Kawada vs Tenryu, Kawada vs Sasaki, Misawa vs Akiyama) this inter-promotional tag match could have easily been overlooked. However, Fuchi/Kawada vs Iizuka/Nagata stands out. *Wrestling Observer* Editor Dave Meltzer gave the match five stars, making it the only match from the year 2000 to receive this rating from one of wrestling's best-known critics. In more recent times, the match has been somewhat forgotten, despite clearly deserving a place in *puroresu* discourse.

Genichiro Tenryu vs Taiyō Kea, 30 July 2002, Nippon Budokan

Genichiro Tenryu was undoubtedly one of the biggest stars in post-split All Japan, helping the company through a crisis when he returned. One of the other wrestlers whose stock rose in the post-split era was Taiyō Kea. With Tenryu well established as one of the biggest stars in Japanese wrestling history, this match served as a passing of the torch and an opportunity for Kea, who later went on to bigger and better things as the future Triple Crown Heavyweight Champion.

The two had previously met in the finals of the 2001 Champion Carnival, where Tenryu had joined the ranks of Triple Crown holders who won while champion. In this rematch, the two exchanged hard shots, with Tenryu making Kea earn everything. It is a wild battle from the beginning, with Tenryu hitting a Giant Baba-esque running neckbreaker to taunt the younger Kea, who was something of a Baba protégé.

Kea looked more certain on his feet in this bout than he did in their Champion Carnival final, while Tenryu took bumps that many younger wrestlers might decline. The match was probably Kea's career best and, at fifteen minutes, stood as a good example of what could be achieved with a more compact match format. It is also a great showcase of how one wrestler (in this case, Tenryu) can help make their opponent seem more important.

Satoshi Kojima vs Genichiro Tenryu, Triple Crown Heavyweight Championship, 17 July 2002, Osaka Jo Hall

This match is worth digging up from both a match quality perspective as well as its historical value. It marks Satoshi Kojima's in-ring debut in All Japan as part of the company's roster, his previous matches having been as part of the New Japan partnership.

Kojima began this stint with the company backing him, as his debut match saw him take on Triple Crown Champion Genichiro Tenryu.

Taking place in a packed Osaka Jo Hall, the match also stood out as a testament to how crowd responses can enhance a match, with the audience's clapping and foot stomping sounding like a downpour had begun. From his entrance at the match's beginning, Satoshi Kojima was treated like a star, with the fans chanting his name (Eastern Lariat Podcast, 2021).

The match told the story of Kojima working to fight to be taken seriously by the more experienced Tenryu, whose selling and facial expressions conveyed that he did not always take this new challenger seriously. By the end of the match, however, he appeared to begrudgingly give Kojima his due.

The match was praised at the time that it took place, with the *Wrestling Observer* Editor Dave Meltzer awarding it ****3/4.

In terms of the match's significance, it marked a transition from the days of Giant Baba's vision for the promotion (still physically represented by a poster of the company founder) to Keiji Mutoh's more sports entertainment aligned Pro Wrestling Love presentation[146].

Satoshi Kojima, one of the stars that left New Japan

with Mutoh, went on to an eight-year run with the promotion. This match went some way towards establishing him as a star in All Japan. At the time, the intention was to make him one of a new core four, alongside Mutoh, Kawada, and Tenryu. While this did not quite come to fruition, the intent is visible.

In this regard, it is worth noting that this match stands out as one of the classic post-split Triple Crown title matches that does not contain any of the 'original' Four Pillars.

ACKNOWLEDGEMENT

No book happens in complete isolation, and I have been helped by a few core people who supported this project.

First, and foremost, my wife Sarah Willett-Foye supported me in this project, encouraging me to undertake it in the first place, reading over the manuscript, and hearing my constant discussions about it. Every project I undertake has enjoyed her support, kindness, and deep reservoir of patience.

Fumi Saito is another person who was key to this project. As well as his excellent foreword, his interview was long and detailed and he was always available to provide feedback. Fumi is someone who hopes to pass on his experience, and he has a wealth of knowledge. As well as his interview, his podcasts *Pacific Rim* and *Write That Down* were both useful as background sources.

Mohammed Yassin is the artist responsible for *Ganbaru*'s cover. He was gracious in allowing me to use this image. You can see more of his work via his website, https://mushkilah.com/.

Hisame answered some important questions for me about Pro Wrestling NOAH. Her contributions to making Japanese pro wrestling accessible for Western fans through the *Puroresu Translation* blog cannot be stated enough.

Another translator, Chris Charlton, was also gracious in answering some questions on the subject of Japanese to English translation. His books, *Lion's Pride* and *Eggshells*, were also sources that I returned to repeatedly.

Richard Aslinger is another person who responded to questions. His prior interviews were a rare look into *puroresu* from a Westerner who was there through some of the key years of its history. I appreciate his responses and his willingness to explain what life was like for those on the other side of the curtain.

Katherine Growcott read through one of the book's many drafts, offering feedback and encouragement. Without knowing how readers would respond to this material, I would have been lost.

My friend and mentor Paul Ryder looked at the manuscript in one of the early draft stages, offering feedback and encouragement.

Oscar and Conrad Bem are two friends I bounced ideas off, discussed approaches with, and drew inspiration from. They were particularly helpful during the latter portion of the draft process. Oscar also helped this project by providing a close eye over the book late in the project, providing detailed editing suggestions. The book would not be the same if not for his help during this process.

My friend Dave De Leon was someone I bounced ideas off. His podcast, *Suwama's Station*, was also a source of much information about the split. Dave also runs the All Japan Trivia Pro Trivia competition on Facebook, which is a great place to learn about the promotion's history and to discuss it with likeminded fans.

Finally, I am grateful to anyone who has taken the time to read this book. Regardless of what group of readers you fall into, I hope it has taught you something about *puroresu* or entertained you.

GLOSSARY

Ace: The top star of a wrestling company, whom the promoter relies upon.

Basement dropkick: A low-angle dropkick to the opponent's legs.

Booker: A member of a wrestling organisation who determines what matches go on the card, how they finish, what wrestlers become champions, and the company's overall storyline direction. Bookers may be wrestlers themselves, as Misawa was in All Japan.

Bump: The act of a wrestler landing flat on their back, attempting to evenly distribute their weight so as to avoid injury. All Japan's King's Road style featured spectacular and sometimes dangerous bumps, such as those taken on the ring apron.

Catch wrestling: A form of wrestling that was popular in the late 19th and early 20th century, catch wrestling eventually led to the creation of professional wrestling. Some of the famous practitioners include Randy Couture, Karl Gotch, and US President Abraham Lincoln.

Chanko: A broth traditionally consumed by professional wrestlers and sumo veterans. It is generally one of the trainees' roles to prepare *chanko*.

Chop: A strike where the wrestler delivering the move swings their arm and lands their forearm on their opponent's body, usually on their chest.

Count out: When a wrestler exits or is knocked outside the ring, the referee will count. In All Japan, the wrestler has ten seconds to re-enter the ring, before he loses the match via count out. This type of finish is considered by fans to be inconclusive and unsatisfying.

Dropkick: A jumping kick, where the wrestler delivering the move leaves their feet.

Emerald Frosion: A move innovated by Mitsuharu Misawa, the Emerald Frosion sees a wrestler hold their opponent over their shoulder, before turning them slightly and dropping them down to the mat.

Enzuigiri: A move where the wrestler delivers a jumping kick to the back of their opponent's head.

Face: A 'good guy' wrestler, intended to be cheered by the fans. Sometimes also known as a 'babyface.'

Gaijin: A foreigner or 'outsider' in Japan. Within *puroresu*, the *gaijin* oftentimes plays a traditional heel role.

Ganso bomb: A dangerous move that sees a wrestler pick their opponent up in a powerbomb position and drape them, before dropping them on their head and shoulders. The move was innovated accidentally by Toshiaki Kawada in a 1999 match against Mitsuharu Misawa. After Kawada broke his arm, he was unable to lift his opponent fully for a powerbomb, implementing the *ganso* bomb instead.

Getting over: Drawing a visible reaction from fans.

Going over: Being the wrestler booked to win the match.

Heel: A 'bad guy' wrestler, intended to elicit boos. The heel role is generally more subtle in puroresu, but the heel role is nonetheless important.

Joshi: A Japanese word for female wrestling.

Kayfabe: The art of maintaining the illusion that professional wrestling is a legitimate contest. The term can refer to wrestlers preventing fans from knowing the inner workings of the business, so as to enhance their enjoyment of the events. While the days of strict kayfabe are considered finished in the West, Japanese wrestling still engages in kayfabe to a certain extent.

Kohei: The newer wrestler, who learns from the more tenured wrestler, especially in a wrestling dojo. The term originates from sumo wrestling traditions.

Konbibi: A convenience store.

Lariat: A hard clothesline, where a wrestler sticks their arm out and strikes their opponent with it. The move was particularly popularised by American wrestler Stan Hansen.

Mid-card: The centre portion of a wrestling event, usually featuring wrestlers who are yet to ascend the main event picture.

Moonsault: An arial move, where a wrestler performs a backflip off the top rope and lands on their opponent.

Neckbreaker: A brutal-looking move where a wrestler turn their opponents head as they drive their body into the mat.

Northern Lights Bomb: A finishing move invented by Akira Hokuto and later used by her husband Kensuke Sasaki and Genichiro Tenryu. The wrestler lifts their opponent from a front facelock position, turns them over, and plants them on the mat, with their opponent taking a back bump. Tenryu used the move at the conclusion of a year 2000 match where he won the Triple Crown.

Pinfall: A popular finishing method, a pinfall occurs when a wrestler's shoulders are held against the mat for three seconds. Wrestlers often 'kick out' as the referee's count reaches two, so as to create more drama for the match.

Potato: When a wrestler unexpectedly throws a hard punch at their opponent, it is sometimes referred to as 'potatoing' them.

Powerbomb: A wrestling move where one wrestler tucks their opponent's head between their knees, before picking them up in a vertical position and dropping them down to the mat. The opponent on the receiving end takes a back bump.

Produce shows: One-off events produced by certain wrestlers or promoters. Motoko Baba ran a produce show in 2005, a few years after she left the professional wrestling industry.

Promoter: The person responsible for operating a professional wrestling organisation.

Promotion: The name given to a professional wrestling group.Selling: When a wrestler makes it look like they are hurt, or display emotion in response to the in-ring action, they are 'selling'.

Senpai: The senior wrestler in a pair.

Shoot: An unplanned event, such as a real-life fight. Exchanges where wrestlers break kayfabe and talk about backstage events are sometimes called 'shoot' interviews.

Stable: A group of wrestlers who band together and team with one another, often with common colours or matching gear.

Stiff: In professional wrestling, a 'stiff' punch, kick, or strike is one that lands hard on an opponent.

Stretch Plum: A submission move used by Toshiaki

Kawada, the Stretch Plum sees a wrestler lift a grounded opponent's head off the mat and place their forearm around that opponent's face, while pulling their arm back. The move was invented by the late Plum Mariko.

Submit: When a wrestler gives up due to being placed in a painful hold. Submission can happen verbally or by the wrestler 'tapping out'.

Suplex: A popular move in Japanese pro wrestling, a suplex is a move where a wrestler throws their opponent. Variations include a vertical suplex (where a wrestler stands up straight and holds their opponents overhead) and a German suplex (where a wrestler throws their opponent from behind).

Tag team: A team (usually) consisting of two wrestlers, who participate in tag matches. During these contests, two teams of two face off, with one wrestler representing each in the ring at any given time. Wrestlers tag in and out.

Tiger Driver: A powerbomb where the wrestler delivering the move lands in a seated pinning position. The move is named for Tiger Mask, and was used by Mitsuharu Misawa since he was the second tiger mask.

Tiger Driver '91: A more dangerous variation of the Tiger Driver, this move sees the wrestler receiving the move take a high bump on their head and shoulders.

Work: Where an event has been planned as part of a wrestling show, that can be called a 'work.'

WORKS CITED

Matt Alt (2020). *Pure Invention: How Japan's Pop Culture Conquered the World*. London: Brown Book Group.

Kagehiro Asano (1999). *SWS Gensou to Jitsuzou*. Tokyo: Nippon Sports Publishing.

Freddie Blassie with Keith Elliot Greenberg (2003). *Listen Here, You Pencil Neck Geeks*. New York: Simon & Schuster.

Aaron Boulding, 'Virtual Pro Wrestling (Import)' [21 March 2000]. IGN. Online: http://ign64.ign.com/articles/161/161131p1.html

Chris Charlton (2015). *Lion's Pride: The Turbulent History of New Japan Pro Wrestling*. San Bernardino: Indiegogo.

Matt Charlton (2020). *J-Crowned: An Illustrated Guide to the Champions of Japanese Wrestling*. Alabama: Hybrid Shoot.

Wayne Daly, 'Suwama takes on executive role with All Japan Pro Wrestling' [9 March 2021]. WrestlingNews.net. Online: https://www.wrestlingnews.net/suwama-takes-on-executive-role-with-all-japan-pro-wrestling/163301/

De Leon, D., & Sarpraicone, M. (Hosts). (2020, November 20). Suwama's Station (No. 5) [Audio podcast episode]. Chairshot Radio Network. https://music.amazon.co.uk/podcasts/1dbd7481-1e92-4bb8-8d4a-964f16e107e0/episodes/45d4fff7-6e93-42a1-be13-083531976030/chairshot-radio-network-suwama's-station-5---taiyo-kea-interview-part-1

De Leon, D., & Sarpraicone, M. (Hosts). (2020, December 24). Suwama's Station (No. 6) [Audio podcast episode]. Chairshot Radio Network. https://www.youtube.com/watch?v=DhgvUCGQ09M

De Leon, D., & Sarpraicone, M. (Hosts). (2021, August 20). Suwama's Station (No. 11) [Audio podcast episode]. Chairshot Radio Network. https://www.youtube.com/watch?v=vMeQe2_WlM8&t=8910s

Mick Foley (1999). *Have A Nice Day: A Tale of Blood and Sweatsocks*. Sydney: HarperCollins.

Mick Foley (2007). *The Hardcore Diaries*. New York: Simon & Schuster.

Fox, D., & Strigga (Hosts). (2021, August 11). Week of Lariat: Satoshi Kojima #3 [Audio podcast episode]. Patreon. https://www.patreon.com/m/2597063/posts

Fox, D., & Hisame (Hosts). (2020, January 10). Senshu Shōkai: An Introduction to Pro Wrestling Noah w/Dylan & Hisame [Audio podcast episode]. Patreon. https://www.patreon.com/posts/senshu-shokai-to-33003571

Helio Fred Garcia, (2017). *Strategic choices for managing potential crises.* Strategy & Leadership, 45(6), 34-40.

Stan Hansen (2014). *The Last Outlaw.* Gallatin: Crowbar Press [Kindle version].

Bret Hart (2007). *Hitman.* Canada: Random House.

Hisame, 'Green Guide to the History of Pro Wrestling NOAH' [23 February 2018]. Online: https://puroprogramtranslations.blogspot.com/2018/02/noah-green-guide-to-history-of-pro.html?fbclid=IwAR21m5HcmDs2WCAYuEKd-HuyD32Sq_3o2ExDQAT4uT28pT_-9gbVsFZDGl70

Hisame, 'Four Days in April: All Japan, NOAH, and Their Troubled History' [27 April 2018]. Online: https://puroprogramtranslations.blogspot.com/2018/04/article.html?fbclid=IwAR3nFeMgh9PH7YE-vymsmH029Ea_vNfWQxldwdfRohtgheP-w9_M6m8iUjKM

Hisame, '(NOAH) Inheriting the Spirit: The story of Eddie Edwards, Kenoh and the GHC Heavyweight

Tite' [2 June 2018]. Online: http://puroprogramtranslations.blogspot.com/2018/06/noah-inheriting-spirit-story-of-eddie.html

Tim Hornbaker (2006). *National Wrestling Alliance: The Untold Story of the Monopoly That Strangled Pro Wrestling*. Toronto: ECW Press [Kindle version].

Husney, E. & Eisener, J. (Creators). (2019). Blood & Wire: Onita's FMW [Television Episode]. In *Dark Side of the Ring*. Vice.

Hidetoshi Ichinose, 'Itami no Kachi' [14 October 2015], Futabasha.

IGN Staff, 'Twenty-Five Wrestlers, led by Mitsuharu Misawa, leave All Japan Pro Wrestling!' [21 June 2000]. Online: https://www.ign.com/articles/2000/06/21/twenty-five-wrestlers-led-by-mitsuharu-misawa-leave-all-japan-pro-wrestling

Case Lowe, 'A retrospective of Violence: The Legacy of Genichiro Tenryu' [16 May 2020]. Voices of Wrestling. Online: https://www.voicesofwrestling.com/2020/05/19/a-retrospective-of-violence-the-legacy-of-genichiro-tenryu/

Mat Lindsay, 'King's Road: The Rise and Fall of All Japan Pro Wrestling—Part 1' [15 August 2016]. Online: https://vulturehound.co.uk/2016/08/kings-road-the-rise-and-fall-of-all-japan-pro-wrestling-part-1/

Mat Lindsay, 'King's Road: The Rise and Fall of All Japan Pro Wrestling—Part 2' [21 August 2016]. Online: https://vulturehound.co.uk/2016/08/kings-road-the-rise-and-fall-of-all-japan-pro-wrestling-part-2/

Itsuki Marui, 'Last Bump' [30 July 2010]. Baseball Magazine Sha.

Dave Meltzer [Editor], 'May 15, 2000, Observer Newsletter: WCW Slamboree Review, Drug Testing in NY, More' [15 May 2000]. Online: https://members.f4wonline.com/wrestling-observer-newsletter/may-15-2000-wrestling-observer-newsletter-wcw-slamboree-review-drug

Dave Meltzer [Editor], 'May 22, 2000, Observer Newsletter: Jumbo Tsuruta Passes Away, ECW Hardcore Heaven Review, More' [22 May 2000]. Online: https://members.f4wonline.com/wrestling-observer-newsletter/may-22-2000-wrestling-observer-newsletter-jumbo-tsuruta-passes-away

Dave Meltzer [Editor], 'June 26, 2000, Observer Newsletter: Birth of NOAH, Vince Russo quits WCW, Tons of news' [26 June 2000]. Online: https://members.f4wonline.com/wrestling-observer-newsletter/june-26-2000-wrestling-observer-newsletter-birth-noah-vince-russo

Dave Meltzer [Editor], 'September 11, 2000, WCW AND ECW Uncertainty, All Japan/New Japan feud, more' [11 September 2000]. Online: https://

members.f4wonline.com/wrestling-observer-newsletter/september-11-2000-wrestling-observer-newsletter-wcw-and-ecw

Dave Meltzer [Editor], 'October 16, 2000, Observer Newsletter: Potential WCW sale, New Japan vs All Japan, Plus more' [16 October 2000]. Online: https://members.f4wonline.com/wrestling-observer-newsletter/october-16-2000-wrestling-observer-newsletter-potential-wcw-sale-new

Dave Meltzer [Editor], 'October 30, 2000, Observer Newsletter: Death of Yokozuna, Bret Hart leaves WCW, More' [30 October 2000]. Online: https://members.f4wonline.com/wrestling-observer-newsletter/october-30-2000-wrestling-observer-newsletter-death-yokozuna-bret-hart

Dave Meltzer [Editor], 'November 27, 2000, Observer Newsletter: Survivor Series review, Stan Hansen retires, More' [27 November 2000]. Online: https://members.f4wonline.com/wrestling-observer-newsletter/november-27-2000-wrestling-observer-newsletter-survivor-series-review

Dave Meltzer [Editor], 'January 1, 2001, Observer Newsletter: Candidates For Wrestler of the Year, Sakuraba Defeats Another Gracie, More' [1 January 2001]. Online: https://members.f4wonline.com/wrestling-observer-newsletter/january-1-2001-wrestling-observer-newsletter-candidates-wrestler-year

Dave Meltzer [Editor], 'January 29, 2001, Observer Newsletter: Royal Rumble Review, Shawn Micheals to Return, More' [29 January 2001]. Online: https://members.f4wonline.com/wrestling-observer-newsletter/january-29-2001-wrestling-observer-newsletter-royal-rumble-review

Dave Meltzer [Editor], 'February 11, 2002, Observer Newsletter: "Questions Surrounding NJPW Talent Leaving for All Japan, More' [11 February 2002]. Online: https://members.f4wonline.com/wrestling-observer-newsletter/february-11-2002-observer-newsletter-questions-surrounding-njpw-talent

Dave Meltzer [Editor], 'June 22, 2009, Observer Newsletter: Misawa Tragic Death, UFC 99, Trump Angle, TripleMania, Sylvia' [22 June 2009]. Online: https://members.f4wonline.com/wrestling-observer-newsletter/june-22-2009-observer-newsletter-misawa-tragic-death-ufc-99-trump

Dave Meltzer [Editor], 'July 1, 2009, Observer Newsletter: "Part II of Misawa bio, big match history, news updates on TNA, WWE' [1 July 2009]. Online: https://members.f4wonline.com/wrestling-observer-newsletter/july-1-2009-observer-newsletter-part-ii-misawa-bio-big-match-history

Dave Meltzer [Editor], 'July 13, 2009, Observer Newsletter: UFC 100, Biggest Draws by Year, Billy

Red Lyons Bio, WWE Buyrates' [13 July 2009]. Online: https://members.f4wonline.com/wrestling-observer-newsletter/july-13-2009-observer-newsletter-ufc-100-biggest-draws-year-billy-red

Dave Meltzer [Editor], 'April 23, 2018, Observer Newsletter: Former AJPW owner Motoko Baba passes away at 76' [23 April 2018]. Online: https://www.f4wonline.com/japan/former-ajpw-owner-motoko-baba-passes-away-78-256306

Mitsuharu Misawa/Norio Suzuki, 'Funade' [30 September 2004]. Hikari Bunsha.

John Molinaro, 'Misawa knocks All Japan off TV' [19 June 2000]. SLAM! Wrestling. Archived from the original on 22 July 2017. Online: https://web.archive.org/web/20170722234659/http://slam.canoe.com/SlamWrestlingInternational/jun19_misawa.html

Nikkan Sports, 'Mr. Misawa attended 100 people including Kawada and Takayama during the night' [19 June 2009]. Nikkan Sports. Online: https://www.nikkansports.com/battle/news/p-bt-tp0-20090619-508224.html

Nikkan Sports, 26,000 people to Mr. Misawa, a line of tears of 2.4 kg' [5 July 2009]. Nikkan Sports. Online: https://www.nikkansports.com/battle/news/p-bt-tp0-20090705-514336.html

Alex Podgorski, 'All Japan's Four Pillars of Heaven

Set the Standard' [26 July 2017]. SLAM! Wrestling. Online: https://slamwrestling.net/index.php/2017/07/26/all-japans-four-pillars-of-heaven-set-the-standard/

Alex Podgorski, 'For Richard Slinger, Wrestling in Japan Was as Real As It Gets' [24 November 2020]. SLAM! Wrestling. Online: https://slamwrestling.net/index.php/2020/11/24/for-richard-slinger-wrestling-in-japan-was-as-real-as-it-gets/?__cf_chl_jschl_tk__=pmd_VWzYCnjZTm3dqgaJPZ-v4OVcOEdCR7bhJYMXWdp9OIMo-1631366768-0-gqNtZGzNAnujcnBszQol

Jim Ross (2017). *Slobberknocker: My Life in Wrestling*. New York: Simon & Schuster.

Jim Ross (2018). *Under the Black Hat: My Life in WWE and Beyond*. New York: Simon & Schuster.

Saito, F., & Valley, J. (Hosts). (2020, May 6). Pacific Rim: Bridge of Dreams [Audio podcast episode]. Wrestling Observer/Figure Four Online. https://www.f4wonline.com/pacific-rim-pro-wrestling-podcast/pacific-rim-bridge-dreams-310306

Saito, F., & Valley, J. (Hosts). (2021, October 13). Pacific Rim: Onita, FMW, strength of NJPW, your questions [Audio podcast episode]. Wrestling Observer/Figure Four Online. https://www.f4wonline.com/pacific-rim-pro-wrestling-podcast/pacific-rim-onita-fmw-strength-njpw-your-questions-356216

Phil Schneider (2021). *Way of the Blade: 100 of the Greatest Bloody Matches in Wrestling History*. Alabama: Hybrid Shoot.

The Four Pillars [@TheFourPillars1]. (30 June 2020). *When Noah sponsored Kodo Fuyuki's retirement at Differ Ariake on April 14th, 2002, the relationship between All Japan and Noah was so awful that Misawa sent Yoshinari Ogawa to collect Genichiro Tenryu by cab, meaning the GHC Heavyweight champion collected the Triple Crown Champion* [Tweet]. Twitter. https://twitter.com/TheFourPillars1/status/1277623740453527556

The Four Pillars [@TheFourPillars1]. (1 February 2021). *Mrs Baba almost didn't get away with concealing Baba's death. A reporter turned up on her doorstep and said, "I hear Baba has been discharged from the hospital." Despite the scent of incense sticks lit for Baba's soul almost giving her away, she said "Thank you. Mr. Baba is fine"* [Tweet]. Twitter. https://twitter.com/TheFourPillars1/status/1320199978465656835

The Four Pillars [@TheFourPillars1]. (5 September 2021). *He practiced lariats on metal poles and chops on concrete walls.* [Tweet]. Twitter. https://twitter.com/TheFourPillars1/status/1434220999013191680

The Four Pillars [@TheFourPillars1]. (5 September

2021). *Japan's economic miracle came after the hard years of war and occupation when they took their place in overseas commerce by delving into the growing electronics market. It had the added bonus of bringing the fledgling puroresu scene into people's homes.* [Tweet]. Twitter. https://twitter.com/TheFourPillars1/status/1434230460507381762

Kyohei Wada, 'Jinsei ha Oshiete Choudo li' [25 December 2004]. Media Factory.

Yahoo News Japan, 'The way for professional wrestling groups to survive in Corona. Unique management strategy of All Japan Wrestling ... Launched movie department?' [15 December 2020]. Yahoo News Japan. https://news.yahoo.co.jp/articles/b9317b6467c469207e71a12d286c0a0009b6d975

Tarzan Yammamoto, 'Kinken no Henshuchou' [18 June 2010]. Takarajimasha.

Printed in Great Britain
by Amazon